SWEDEN

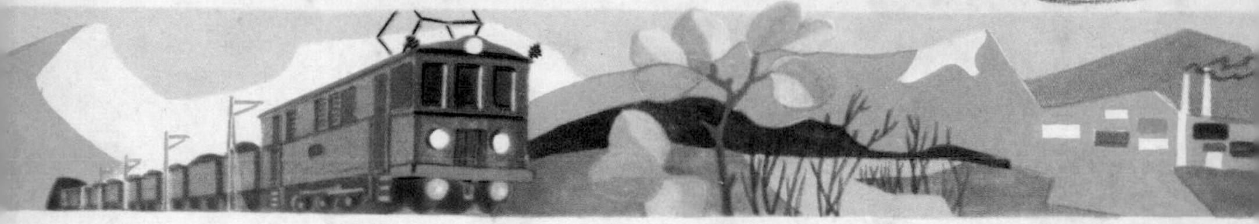

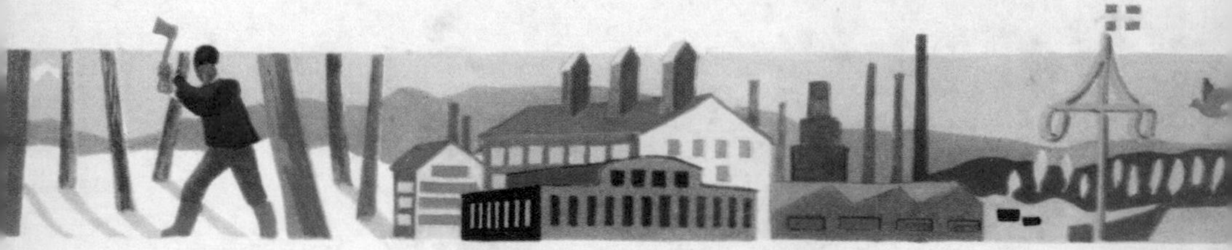

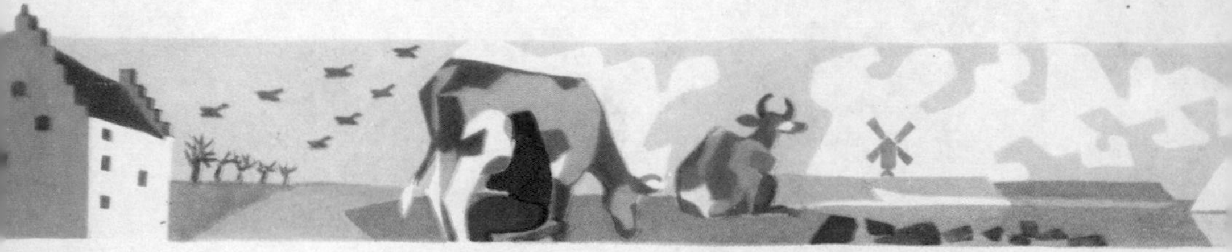

INTRODUCTION TO SWEDEN

INTRODUCTION
TO
SWEDEN

By

INGVAR ANDERSSON

and others

Published by

THE SWEDISH INSTITUTE
STOCKHOLM

◀ FORUM ▶

Translation by
NILS G. SAHLIN ·

Picture editor:
GÖSTA LUNDQUIST

Printed in Sweden by

Almqvist & Wiksells
BOKTRYCKERI AKTIEBOLAG
UPPSALA 1949

TABLE OF CONTENTS

FOREWORD

As indicated by the title, this book aims to serve as an introduction to a study of Sweden. A comprehensive survey is made of the country and its people, its natural resources and economic life, its history and modern society. The text follows a uniform plan and forms a connected story. No claim is advanced, however, in respect to exhaustive or definitive information. Only a general outline is drawn to furnish starting points for further studies, either through personal visits or the pursuit of other books.

The basic material for the book was furnished by Dr. Ingvar Andersson. In some respects it had to be condensed to remain within the scope of the plan; some sections of Dr. Andersson's manuscript have been expanded and brought up to date. For this additional work we are indebted primarily to Professor Gunnar Heckscher, Dr. Gustaf Hilleström, Mr. Sture Petrén, Mr. Hans Risberg, and Mr. Lars-Erik Thunholm. Other experts have contributed information on a variety of matters. Aside from a couple of brief passages, the chapter on the Press in Sweden is based on a longer article by Professor Herbert Tingsten in *Nordisk demokrati.* The chapter on The Church is written by Mr. Erik Sandberg. The editorial work was done at the Swedish Institute in Stockholm by Dr. Bertil Nydahl, and the translation by Dr. Nils G. Sahlin, director and curator of the American Institute of Swedish Arts, Literature and Science in Minneapolis, Minnesota, U. S. A. The pictorial material was edited by Mr. Gösta Lundquist, the statistical material by Mr. Gustaf Holmstedt.

Introduction to Sweden is published at the request of the Ministry for Foreign Affairs and replaces its *Sweden Year-Book,* the latest edition of which appeared in 1938. It should be mentioned here that the Swedish Institute plans to publish a number of smaller pamphlets, each dealing with a special field or subject and intended to complement the present volume. Several have already appeared in print and are listed in the Bibliography.

Nils Holgersson is the hero of the famous book by Selma Lagerlöf. The picture shows the start of *The Wonderful Adventures of Nils*. The thumbling begins the journey over Sweden on the gander's back from the shore of Skåne. The wild geese are over the water. Part of a drawing by Sven Erixson. (In the public elementary school at Olovsund.)

THE LAND AND THE PEOPLE

SURVEY OF BACKGROUND

SIZE AND CLIMATE

MOUNTAINS AND SOIL

PROVINCES AND TOWNS

Götaland

Svealand

Norrland

LANGUAGE AND POPULATION

SURVEY OF BACKGROUND

Sweden has been characterized as "a modern democracy on ancient foundations," and this phrase undoubtedly carries an essential point. Sweden's democracy is quite modern in its manifestations, and her liberty has ancient traditions. The social system has been greatly implemented and expanded during the past few decades, but it is based on a long historical development. Slavery was abolished in Sweden back in the fourteenth century, and no attempts to deprive the people of their liberty were successful even during the time when serfdom of the peasants was general on the Continent. Many of the country's traditions are still vital influences, its culture is based on old foundations, and the basic concepts of its constitution are time-honored.

The Swedish social system and cultural life have to a large extent developed from their native backgrounds. Foreign influences normally reached Sweden late and then only as aftermaths of the European trends.

Until comparatively recently the country remained an outpost in the geographical sense. The group of adventurous Swedes who over three hundred years ago landed with their two ships on the shore of present-day Delaware had a journey behind them which had consumed four months. Even a

11

hundred years ago the emigrant ships took from eight to nine weeks for the passage to America.

The air age in which we live has miraculously altered Sweden's location. Stockholm and Paris are a mere six hours apart; the great circle route from New York to Moscow crosses Sweden about two hundred miles north of Stockholm. Great liners reach the Swedish west coast in ten days or less from the United States; the airlines whisk the traveler across the Atlantic overnight. Modern polar projection maps indicate not only that Sweden is nearer the rest of the world than formerly seemed to be the case but also that she serves as an important transit point for much of today's global air traffic.

Typically Swedish are the deep forests and power-producing streams, the patches and plains which for centuries have yielded the people their hard-earned crops. But in Sweden, as in other countries, agriculture has lost its rank as the chief occupation of the people. Industrialization took place somewhat later than in other parts of Europe, but its progress was instead more rapid in Sweden than elsewhere. Many products of Swedish industry are known the world over, and foreign trade is actually one of the most important links in the country's relations with the rest of the world. Under normal conditions every country is included in the commercial contacts.

In Anglo-American accounts of World War II the name of Bofors, the large Swedish arms manufacturing concern, is frequently encountered. AGA automatic beacons, made in Sweden, are found on all the seven seas; Swedish telephones ring in almost every part of the globe; and Swedish matches are one of the best known international commodities.

Swedish pulp, one of the country's most important products, is shipped everywhere. A Swedish industrialist made the following comment about it shortly before the recent war:

"It travels to California and returns to Sweden as tissue

12

around fragrant oranges; to Yokohama and becomes colored lanterns; to Buenos Aires for conversion into imitation leather; to Philadelphia, where it is turned into cartons, cement bags, rugs, and fishing lines; to the Thames and becomes newsprint; as basic material to the rayon-stocking mills in Genoa; and to the factories in Rouen, where molded toys are made."

Goods unloaded in Swedish ports come from every corner of the earth: raw materials, such as cotton, hemp, and flax for the textile mills; soybean oil for margarine manufacture; coffee in great quantities to satisfy the national preference in beverages; machinery, motor cars, nylons. Two of the most vital prerequisites for Sweden's economic activity, coal and oil, must be imported from abroad. Brisk commercial activity is characteristic of modern Sweden. On the whole, Sweden is more dependent than most countries on her foreign trade.

But Sweden also has important cultural contacts with other countries. Her contribution to the world of scientists, scholars, authors, and artists is considerable; in Sweden those from abroad are met with understanding and esteem. Sweden's cultural life is much exposed to influences and impressions from abroad. Literature and films in English and other foreign tongues find eager audiences, language studies are popular, the members of the professions keep themselves informed of progress abroad. Evidence of contact is also found in numerous other connections. In Sinclair Lewis' *Martin Arrowsmith* we encounter a vividly drawn character who is a Swede and in Willa Cather's novels we frequently find descendants of Swedish immigrants. August Strindberg, the Swedish playwright, undoubtedly exerted an influence on Shaw and O'Neill. The fame of some outstanding Swedish women has spread as far as the United States: Fredrika Bremer, novelist, author of travel descriptions from America, and feminist; Ellen Key, societal philosopher and writer; Selma Lagerlöf, Nobel Prize winner

13

and world-famed author; Elsa Beskow, fairy tale writer; and film stars, such as Greta Garbo and Ingrid Bergman.

A noted symbol of the intellectual contacts between Sweden and the rest of the world is the Nobel Prizes. They were established toward the end of the last century by Alfred Nobel, inventor of dynamite and other explosives. The income from the Nobel fund is distributed annually to "those who during the past year have rendered humanity the greatest service" through scientific discoveries (physics, chemistry, and medicine), creative literary work, and the furtherance of world peace. According to the donor's will, no regard is paid to the candidate's nationality; another significant proviso is that the Peace Prize be made by the parliament of Norway, at that time and until 1905 united with Sweden.

For nearly three centuries Sweden has been without colonial domains. New Sweden, the territory surrounding the present city of Wilmington, Delaware, was settled by Swedes and Finns in 1638, but the sovereignty was soon lost to the Dutch. Finland, lost to the Russians in 1809, had since the twelfth century been an integral part of the Swedish kingdom. The final remnant of colonial possession was the island of St. Bartholomew in the West Indies, sold to France in 1877 after scarcely a century of Swedish rule.

Sweden has no minority problem within its boundaries and no ambitions for expansion without. The country has been at peace with her neighbors for more than 130 years. But the Swedes as individuals are adventurous travelers. Many have settled in every part of the world and made notable economic and intellectual contributions to the countries which have welcomed them.

Swedish engineers, businessmen, and workers have played a significant role in many parts of the world. They have helped build factories and power plants in Russia, railroads and bridges in Turkey and Iran. Swedish officers, physicians, teachers, and other experts are once more helping Haile Selassie create a new Ethiopia, 140 being in the service of the Ethiopian government in 1947. Most striking is the migratory movement to the United States which took place in the second half of the nineteenth century. By 1890 nearly half a million native Swedes were settled in America, and this number has since remained approximately constant (1940: 445 070). Inclusion of the second generation brings the number of inhabitants of Swedish descent in the United States up to about one and a half million.

These residents have done their share in building America. Several of New York's and especially Chicago's skyscrapers have to some degree risen under the hands of Swedish builders and craftsmen, and so have thousands of private homes; the great Greyhound transportation network has a Swede at its head; the Matson Line, organized by a former Swedish sea captain, is one of the largest on the Pacific coast; one of Ford's precision experts was a Swede; men of Swedish parentage sit in the United States Congress; Carl Sandburg, Charles A. Lindbergh, Edgar Bergen are random names of nationally known, second generation American Swedes. In the course of the years Swedish immigrants and their children have brought under cultivation an estimated ten million acres in the United States, an area equal to all the arable land in Sweden.

Swedish explorers have probed the far-away, uncharted spots on our maps. In the eighteenth century some disciples of Karl von Linné (Linnaeus) accompanied Captain Cook on his travels around the world and penetrated deeper into the Antarctic than anyone else prior to such modern explorers as Shackleton, Amundsen, and Byrd. Some of Linné's other students undertook extensive journeys all over the globe. Later scientific travelers from Sweden made notable contributions. A. E. Nor-

15

denskiöld was the first to clear the Northeast Passage (1878—1879), making possible the circumnavigation of the Old World.

The first attempt to fly to the North Pole was made by a Swede, S. A. Andrée, whose balloon went down in the arctic wastes in 1897. Sven Hedin is famed as the explorer of Tibet, making his first expedition in 1894—1897, his last in 1938. Sten Bergman was one of the first scientists to investigate Kamtchatka.

This activity has had its counterpart in domestic endeavors, and Sweden has been able to gain a high measure of economic security, even a certain affluence, at least by European standards. The country which in 1632 hesitated to invite foreign representatives to the funeral of its fallen king, fearing that "they will see how poor we are," today welcomes guests from abroad and encourages them to observe and write, if they choose, without restriction.

We shall attempt to show in the following chapters how this has come about and in so doing give an account of the natural resources placed at the disposal of Sweden's inhabitants.

SIZE AND CLIMATE

A circle drawn with Trälleborg, Sweden's southernmost town as the center and begun at Treriksröset in the far north where Finland, Norway, and Sweden meet would pass slightly east of Moscow, touch Naples and almost the Spanish-French boundary to the south, and skirt the southwestern coast of Ireland. Clearly Sweden is a large European country; superimposed upon the United States its extremes would reach from Washington, D. C., to the southern tip of Florida.

1. Typically Swedish scenery. Photo by Gösta Lundquist.

2 and 3. Wide divergencies in climate and scenery exist among the various parts of a country as extensive as Sweden. In Skåne the climate resembles that of Central Europe, the winter lasting about two months. In good years, peaches, mulberries, and walnuts ripen here. Above: View from the plains of Skåne with a field of ripe rye and, left, a beech forest in the central part of the province. Photos by Bertil Norberg and Frans Malmros.

4 and 5. In some parts of northern-most Sweden, on the barren tundras and up in the high mountain terrains, the winter is eight months long. During the short but intensive summer the sun shines night and day for two months, and an almost luxuriant flora springs up in these arctic regions. High up on the mountain slopes the plants may reach the height of a man, and in the valleys (right) the bush willow thickets become nearly impenetrable. Above: View toward "Lapp Gate" (*Lapp-porten*) near Abisko, internationally known tourist center. Photos by Valentin Hagerth and Gösta Lundquist.

6. View of a region in the province of Östergötland, in many ways typical of a country which boasts no less than 96,000 lakes, forests covering more than half of its area, and a scanty tenth of its surface for tilled soil. Photo by Gösta Lundquist.

7. Göteborg, gateway to the West, the country's second city and most important export harbor. Photo by K. W. Gullers.

8 and 9. Long stretches of the Swedish coast are frayed into extensive archipelagoes. The lower picture shows a typical fishing village on the west coast and (at top) a fjord landscape on the Gulf of Bothnia, archipelago of Ångermanland province. Photos by Gunvor Ahlberg and Oscar Bladh.

10 and 11. In a northern country like Sweden, spring and summer — vacation time for most Swedes — are joyously anticipated seasons. Upper picture opposite page: Students in Uppsala greet the arrival of spring on Walpurgis Night, April 30th. Below: July regatta in the Stockholm archipelago. Photos by O. Sagerholm and Oscar Norberg.

12. Midsummer holiday in Leksand, province of Dalarna. Photo by Olof Ekberg.

13. Many of the pleasant, small towns in Sweden are very old and have a fascinating historical background. Most remarkable among them is Visby on the island of Gotland, which annually attracts more than 60,000 visitors, a greater number than the population of the whole island. Northern Gate (*Norderport*), Visby. Photo by Artur Larsson.

14 and 15. Norrtälje in the province of Uppland, a typical Swedish small town with the church in the center and neat wooden cottages lining the streets. Right: Ystad in Skåne, with half-timbered houses along the medieval, meandering streets. Photos by Bo Törngren and Folke Nyström.

16. Selma Lagerlöf called Stockholm "the city that swims on the waters". View of the Old City and the South (*Södermalm*) from the City Hall tower. Photo by Gösta Lundquist.

17 and 18. Forests and more forests meet the eye of the traveler in Sweden. In large parts of the country the inhabited and cleared areas are only small patches in the green ocean of the woods. A small farm at Kilsbergen in the province of Närke, and an elk in a forest marsh, Södermanland. Photos by Erik Israelsson and Carl Odelberg.

19. Next to the forests the rivers with their rapids and falls are the most significant basis for Sweden's economic life. A glimpse of the great Harsprånget (Hare's Leap) waterfall. Photo by Gösta Lundquist.

20 and 21. About one seventh of the country's area is mountain territory with large wastelands. Here during the summer the Lapps roam with their herds of reindeer, but large numbers of tourists also find their way into these regions. Above: A Lapp hut in Akkajaure and, letf, a Lapp woman. Photos by Gösta Lundquist.

Sweden's 173 347 square miles rank her fifth among the large countries of Europe; only France, Germany, Russia, and Spain have larger area. Twenty states the size of Sweden would approximate the area of continental United States.

In its contours the country is not unlike California, the area of Sweden being about ten percent larger. But Sweden's capital, Stockholm, lies on the latitude of northern Labrador, the Arctic Circle passes through in the north, and the country cannot boast a Californian climate. However, because of the warm currents carried to Scandinavia by the Gulf Stream, Sweden's climate is surprisingly mild. The mean annual temperature ranges from 27°F. in the north to 45°F. in the south. Stockholm's mean temperature indicates that the city is cooler than New York both in winter and summer.

Wide divergencies in climate naturally exist among the various parts of a country as extensive as Sweden. The southern end averages only 56 days annually with a mean temperature under the freezing point; farthest north this number rises to 217. In warm years walnuts, grapes, peaches, and mulberries ripen down south; the northern provinces cultivate hardy varities of barley, wheat, and certain vegetables. Because of the long summer days in the north and with the help of modern cross-breeding, Norrland (North Land) is making gradual progress toward the successful raising of crops and fruits formerly thought impossible there.

Scattered habitations have existed in Norrland since prehistoric times, but not until about a century ago did this part of the country really begin to be developed. A Swedish pioneer spirit akin to that of America's frontier has prompted the people to penetrate the wilderness up to the very foot of the forbidding mountain ranges. The northern half of the country is inhabited by only twelve percent of the total population but possesses tremendous economic values because of its resources in forests and metal ores. Ancient Sweden still has regions to conquer and room for development. This inspires the inhabitants to undertake new ventures, to continue exploring the wilderness and make new discoveries. Both for the nation and the individuals the reward is greater material well-being.

MOUNTAINS AND SOIL

Barren mountains are found only in the region farthest to the northwest in Sweden, and they bear no comparison with those of Switzerland or Norway. Nevertheless, it is fairly easy to gain a conception of the groundmass on which the country rests. A geographer has pointed out that it is conveniently studied by examining some of the notable buildings in Sweden. The primary rock, mostly gray granite, was used rather rough-hewn in the building of some of the oldest stone churches in central Sweden, which contributed to their distinctive, severe appearance. In modern times the stonecutting industry has produced excellent building materials from Swedish granite in all its fine hues. Outstanding examples are the red granite of the House of Parliament and the blue-gray granite in the colonnade of Stockholm's Concert Hall. Granite and gneiss lie at the surface in the archipelagoes and many other places; from them originated the gravel, rubblestone, and lean soil found in various parts of the country. Another primary rock is the leptite. While not used for construction, it has, nevertheless, determined the settling of considerable regions in Sweden, for this and related rocks contain most of the country's ore, yielding iron, copper, silver, and gold.

Other deposits on top of the bedrock exist, but they are found in few and limited regions, where they remain at all, most of them having been worn away. There are, however, Silurian deposits in places, containing slate, sandstone, and limestone. They, too, can be studied in the public buildings. As examples may be mentioned the Lund Cathedral in southern Sweden, built of sandstone in the twelfth century; the beautiful Gotland churches of limestone from that island; Vadstena's famous abbey, constructed of bluish limestone from the province of Östergötland; the venerable church at Husaby, built of sandstone from Västergötland; and many others. These buildings also indicate to a certain extent the location of the Silurian deposits, from which fertile soil has been formed. The main areas of this type include the islands of Öland and Gotland, the province of Skåne, the plains in the provinces of Östergötland, Västergötland, Närke, and certain parts of Dalarna and Jämtland.

There are no deposits from the next few geological periods, and hence none from the Carboniferous. Sweden's only supply of fossil fuel exists in a few minor coal deposits in northwestern Skåne from the Triassic and Jurassic periods. The Cretaceous period left traces in southern Skåne. However, in the greater part of the country the most recent deposits lie directly on the primary rock and have been formed from it in the course of millions of years as the rock disintegrated into rubblestone, gravel, and sand. These lean soils place their stamp on most of the country. Their evolution is remarkable, relatively recent, and carefully investigated by the geologists.

The various geological formations thus provide the very basis for the country and the life of its people. The primary rock in some regions contains valuable ores. Lean soils produced from the disintegration of the primary rock by natural forces cover the greater part of Sweden's forested regions. The Silurian rocks, partly pulverized into good earth, are found in relatively small and scattered areas. In the south, finally, are the scanty, hard coal deposits. This, then, is literally the foundation at man's disposal in Sweden. Lack of coal and oil must, however, be considered a serious deficiency in Sweden's economic life and an obstacle to her self-sufficiency, if again cut off from the rest of the world. This was particularly noticeable during the war years and has even caused difficulties since then.

HIGHWAYS TO SWEDEN

The most important approaches to Sweden have always been by water. More than half of the boundary, over 1500 miles, is coastline. Travelers from the west first meet the outer, barren rocks of Bohuslän province, then the larger, inhabited islands, and finally arrive at Sweden's largest ocean port, Göteborg (*yû'tĕ·bŏr'y'*; Gothenburg). The approach from the east or southeast is less austere, for the seven thousand islands in the Stockholm archipelago are for the most part green and friendly. Southern sea lanes lead from Denmark to the cities of Malmö and Hälsingborg, from the Continent to the small town of Trälleborg, where the great railroad ferries dock. Here the stranger is greeted by the broad plains of southern Skåne and an open shore. Öresund (The Sound) at its narrowest part looks like a broad river separating Denmark and Sweden. Shakespeare laid the scene of his *Hamlet* here, in the Danish castle of Kronborg near Helsingör (Elsinore), but neither the Danish nor the Swedish coast has any

> "... dreadful summit of the cliff
> That beetles o'er his base into the sea."

"Dreadful summits" are met, however, when the traveler enters Sweden from northern Norway. Railways and roads pick a cautious path through the mountainous terrain and unite the two countries. The snow-capped mountains on the Swedish side are succeeded by a wide forest region notched with river valleys, this in turn by the fertile seaboard on the Gulf of Bothnia. Torneälv (*älv* = river) and Muonioälv form the boundary between Sweden and Finland, and the railway crosses near the mouth of the Torne. But the Swedish coaches do not roll on, for the Finnish railways use the wider, Russian gauge, and a transfer is necessary.

PROVINCES AND TOWNS

The country is divided into three parts: Götaland (Land of the Goths) in the south, Svealand (Land of the Svear, i. e. Swedes) in the middle, and Norrland in the North. Administratively Sweden is portioned into administrative districts *(län)* and the City of Stockholm as a separate unit, but the older division into provinces is of greater historical interest and comes more readily to the Swedish mind. The Swedes prefer to speak in terms of Skåne or Dalarna (Dalecarlia), say, as provinces, irrespective of the district boundaries. Skåne, for example, is divided into two administrative districts; the province of Öland is a part of Kalmar district, which itself is one of three districts in the province of Småland.

Götaland

Skåne is "Sweden's Granary," her southernmost province with the best farmland, where 12 % of the country's population live on 2 ¹/₂ % of the total area. Here the country's largest wheat crop is produced, but the province also boasts large industrial centers. This was the first region in the country to be settled, and a great number of historic structures testify to its past. Most notable are the famous royal grave at Kivik, the Romanesque cathedral in Lund, and the many magnificent castles ranging in time of construction from the fifteenth to the seventeenth century. The people of this province are considered capable and energetic, conscious of their own worth, and well versed in the art of good living.

On the whole Skåne is not a typical Swedish region, but to the north in the province the more characteristic forests begin. Northeast of Skåne lies the province of *Blekinge* with the Karlskrona naval base. *Halland* extends to the northwest with a densely populated, agricultural region in the southern part and numerous resorts along the shore. Largest of Götaland's provinces is *Småland,* by and large a lean and stony territory. Its people are persevering and ingenious. They have started a large number of small-scale industries, such as shops that make traps to catch mice in Australia or wooden clotheshangers, for world-wide export. Småland also has developed some artcraft industries, and the Swedish match industry centers in Jönköping, capital of the province. The world-wide concern with the well-known "Three Stars" for a trade-mark has its home office in this town. Nearby is the town of Huskvarna, famous for its manufacture of shotguns, rifles, and sewing machines. Vättern, a long, deep, mysterious lake claimed by the folk tale to be bottomless and connected under ground with the Lake of Constance, extends from Jönköping about eighty miles to the north. The provinces of Östergötland and Västergötland lie east and west of the lake, respectively.

The points of the compass frequently appear in Swedish placenames and are easy to identify: *norr-, öster-, söder-,* and *väster-* are the combining forms corresponding to north, east, south, and west.

Östergötland is a fertile agricultural region, rich in historical relics. Carved on the famed "Rök Stone" is the longest runic inscription known; Sweden's oldest monastery was located at Alvastra. Vadstena on the Vättern shore was Saint Birgitta's (Bridget's) town and the country's spiritual focus during the fourteenth and fifteenth centuries. Norrköping is the oldest and largest textile manufacturing center.

Västergötland's people have always been known for their excellence in weaving and other homecrafts, for their briskness and business ability. Large textile industries are located around Borås. The "Västgöta Mountains" are rare geological formations which display interesting and varied stratification. All of this region is rich in old traditions.

A narrow strip of Västergötland follows the navigable Göta River on both sides down to the west coast. For centuries this corridor was Sweden's only outlet in that direction, located between Halland, then a Danish possession, and Bohuslän, which belonged to Norway. Many a bitter battle was fought for this strip of land. At the mouth of the river lies Sweden's ocean port and second largest city, *Göteborg*. Her shipyards definitely place Sweden second among the shipbuilding nations. Göteborg is also a thriving manufacturing city, especially for textiles and metal goods.

To the north of Göteborg lies *Bohuslän*, traditionally the province of seafarers, many of whom today engage in deep sea fishing. It should also be mentioned that Bohuslän is richer in rock carvings than any other region. These remarkable instances of primitive art were carved in the rocks during the Bronze Age, about a thousand years before the birth of Christ, for purposes of religion and magic. In the north, Bohuslän adjoins Norway, and farther up, at the boundary, lies the province of *Dalsland,* a scenic Swedish idyl.

Götaland also includes two large islands in the Baltic, *Got-*

land and *Öland,* each a separate province. Both islands rest on a groundmass of limestone; both have an interesting, unusual flora and a mild climate. Gotland's capital is Visby, in the Middle Ages the foremost town in the Hanseatic League and the transit point for trade between the northern countries, Germany, and Eastern Europe. The "City of Roses and Ruins" with its famous tower-studded wall from the thirteenth and fourteenth centuries has remarkably well preserved its medieval character and is a mecca for foreign visitors.

Near Öland's popular resort Borgholm is another famous ruin, located at the edge of Alvaret, a wide limestone tableland of great interest to botanists and artists.

Svealand

Götaland and Svealand are separated by ridges and deep forests. In the old days this boundary region was very difficult to penetrate. Now the main railway lines and comfortable highways traverse these parts. The main provinces of Svealand are grouped around Mälaren, a lake studded with islands and tattered by a thousand bays and straits. To the south of Mälaren lies *Södermanland,* sometimes called Sweden's most typical province. This characterization is based on the scenic beauty of sparkling waters, white birches, rolling hills, and prosperous farms. Many consider this the province where the finest Swedish is spoken. Most notable among its industrial centers is Eskilstuna, famous for the manufacture of metal goods.

North of Lake Mälaren lies the province of *Uppland,* once the political and cultural focus in the old kingdom of the Svear. Powerful and pomp-loving kings resided here, as attested by the huge burial mounds still preserved near the former heathen temple at Gamla (Old) Uppsala. On the remains of this temple the first Christian cathedral in Sweden was built. Uppsala, seat of Sweden's oldest university (1477) and residence of the archbishop, lies in the approximate center of the province.

The coastal regions of Uppland are collectively known as Roslagen and were during the ninth century and later the starting point for viking forays against Russia. In the northern part of the province an excellent iron ore is mined.

Stockholm, the nation's capital and as such the seat of royalty, government, and parliament, is situated where Lake Mälaren overflows into the Baltic Sea. One of the world's most attractively located cities, Stockholm is widely known for its beauty and grace. The city is rich in outstanding examples of fine architecture, old and modern, such as the historic Riddarholm Church, the Royal Palace built by Nicodemus Tessin the Younger in the eighteenth century, Ragnar Östberg's famous City Hall, the Stadium of the 1912 Olympics, the inspiring modern Högalid and Engelbrekt churches, to mention but a few. Stockholm's 3 900 acres of parks are well planned and carefully maintained; it is difficult to pause anywhere without a view toward a park area with trees and flowers or toward a glittering waterway. The opera and the theater flourish; the wide popularity of the modern film is attested by a hundred cinemas, large and small. The industrial world is represented by such internationally known concerns as de Laval Separators, AGA (automatic gas beacons), L. M. Ericsson (telephones), and Elektrolux (refrigerators and vacuum cleaners), with headquarters and factories in the capital or its immediate vicinity.

The iron districts in the provinces west of Lake Mälaren, known collectively as Bergslagen, are a metal belt around the waist of Sweden. Iron mining began here in the thirteenth century, but even prior to that the valuable ore had been gathered from the bottoms of lakes and marshes. The feeling

41

for iron and how to treat it has been handed down among the people from time immemorial. Swedish iron mining and smelting originated in the province of *Västmanland*, but the mining tradition is also strong in the northern parts of the neighboring province of *Närke*. Örebro, province capital of Närke, is a shoe manufacturing center and located on a fertile plain, not in mining territory. Farthest west toward the Norwegian boundary and north of Sweden's largest lake, Vänern, lies the fair province of *Värmland*. This is a classic mining and iron-working region and, furthermore, the province where forestry in the modern sense was first practiced. It is also known in Sweden as the promised land of poetry and imagination. Four of Sweden's chief literary representatives were born in Värmland: Esaias Tegnér (1782—1846), Erik Gustaf Geijer (1783 —1847), Gustaf Fröding (1860—1911), and Selma Lagerlöf (1858—1940). Värmland has become known as the "Gösta Berling Country" after the hero in one of Selma Lagerlöf's best-known novels.

Northernmost of the Svealand provinces is *Dalarna* (Dalecarlia), where ancient folkways, costumes, and architecture still are in evidence. In this historic region with its deeply rooted, artistic and cultural traditions the people have deliberately preserved many aspects of ages past. Perhaps somewhat of a consciously preserved attraction for the foreign visitors is involved here, but the share of genuine tradition is considerable. In the southern part of the province, agriculture and mining industry exist side by side, while in the north the uniquely old-fashioned farming country dominates. Dalarna's center is beautiful Lake Siljan; its environs are famous travel territory both for the Swedes themselves and their guests from abroad. Names such as Rättvik, Leksand, and Mora are rich in tradition; at Mora Anders Zorn, one of Sweden's foremost artists, made his home.

The inhabitants of Dalarna are known for the retention of their distinctive group characteristics. During the sixteenth century, when Sweden as we know it was in a formative stage, the Dalecarlians were the ones who most stubbornly defended the ancient provincial rights and distinctions. They were the ones who in the end rallied around Gustav Vasa (1496—1560), the founder of modern Sweden, recalling him from his flight toward Norway. A sixty-mile ski race, the cross-country "Vasa Run," is held every winter along the path of that unfinished journey.

Bergslagen, Sweden's oldest industrial region, was the hub from which the classic Swedish liberation movements emanated. Leaders in the successful attempts to throw off the foreign yoke were such men as Engelbrekt Engelbrektsson (d. 1436) and Gustav Vasa. As already indicated, many of the most important ironworking and metal industries are now located here, and for Swedish conditions it is a densely inhabited industrial territory. Västerås is the home town of the Swedish Metal Works and of ASEA (*Allmänna Svenska Elektriska Aktiebolaget*, Sweden's General Electric Company, but not connected with the American G E). Large mines, ironworks, and factories, such as Norberg, Grängesberg, and Bofors, are scattered throughout Bergslagen. Forest industries, like the Billerud Company and Mölnbacka-Trysil, are found in the western part, i. e. in the province of Värmland. Especially characteristic of the Swedish industrial tradition are two large concerns which since the distant past have combined forestry and agriculture with iron and wood processing. *Stora Kopparbergs Bergslags Aktiebolag* with home offices in Falun—known in England as "Stora" (Great)—is the world's oldest company still in operation. Its history dates back to the 1280's, and the properties include ironworks like Domnarvet and wood processing plants like Skutskär on the Gulf of

Bothnia coast. The second large concern is the *Uddeholm Company* in Värmland, owner of a number of such ironworks as Hagfors and of the wood product industries at Skoghall, where the Klar River empties into Lake Väner.

Norrland

No conspicuous change in scenery marks the transition from northern Svealand to southern Norrland. Popular winter resorts and barren mountains are found even in upper Dalarna toward the Norwegian boundary. The comparatively low terrain north of Dalälven (Dal River) does not represent an appreciable change; it is merely a continuation of the Bergslagen landscape. But this great river, which holds the long distance record as a timber carrier, is the natural boundary between Norrland and the rest of Sweden.

As the traveler proceeds farther and farther north, he finds himself more and more obviously in the "snow regions." Because of this climatic difference and the distances involved, the Norrland provinces were settled more recently than those of Svealand and Götaland. Norrland was the last part of the country to be colonized, and here a vigorous frontier spirit still prevails. We mentioned above that Norrland actually began to be affected by modern progress only about a hundred years ago. As a result, the provinces in the north are not so differentiated in the public mind as those farther south. They may, to be sure, seem rather like one another when viewed from the speeding train as it passes through the vast forest regions of the interior, divided by the large river valleys, or through the lowlands along the coast. Nevertheless, each province possesses its own, very characteristic features.

Gästrikland, southernmost and smallest of them all, has little more of the northern character than its neighbor to the south, but even here the forest industries, Norrland's chief occupation, are much in evidence. The iron industry also reaches way up here. One of Sweden's best known ironworks, Sandviken, is located in Gästrikland, and at an ironworks in this province the historic event of the first successful Bessemer smelting took place in 1858.

In *Hälsingland*, the next province to the north along the coast, forestry and its industries flourish on the tremendous scale characteristic of modern Norrland. Today a considerable portion of Sweden's life and activity pulsates in these wooded provinces. The immense forests in the upper regions supply the raw material; the network of rivers which combine to create the great Norrland waterways to the coast furnishes water power for electricity and transport channels for the timber; and near the harbors and towns at the mouths of the major rivers lie the huge sawmills and pulp factories. Along the lower part of the Ljusna River and at its mouth we encounter a series of large, industrial communities, such as Bergvik, the Marma Works, and others. The greatest concentration of forest industries is located in the coastal region of *Medelpad*, around the mouths of the Ljunga and Indal rivers. It is "a continuous, densely populated, town-like settlement" north and south of the town of Sundsvall, nearly twenty miles in length along the shore and with a total population of 50 000.

Largest of the great waterways is the Ångerman River, most of which runs through the province of *Ångermanland*. Far up into the river valley extends Ådalen, another large area studded with forest industries, known both for its serious labor conflicts in former days and for its tradition of romance and poetry, the latter perpetuated especially by the Norrland-born author Pelle Molin. Härnösand, in the southern corner, is the capital of the province. Farthest north and in southern *Västerbotten*, the adjacent province, we encounter the Mo and Dom-

45

sjö Works. The companies operating in these industrial regions are among the largest concerns in the country, and under normal conditions many of them engage in world-wide export. Names of factories as well as settlements in many instances indicate the identity of the concerns. In this connection the Swedish Cellulose Company should also be mentioned, a holding company for several of the large factories along the seaboard. Ludvig Nordström, a Swedish author of note, has devoted much of his literary production to the Norrland provinces, especially to Ångermanland. He once called this part of the country "Sweden's Gold Coast," and the expression is undoubtedly justified.

In the interior and along the Norwegian boundary lie two more of the Norrland provinces. *Härjedalen* is the most secluded of all. It has no towns, no modern industry, and the communications are poor. Life in Härjedalen still retains some of the pioneer aspects. To the north lies *Jämtland*. The central portion of this province is Sweden's northernmost, first-rate agricultural area, a fertile Silurian region which has fostered a population of individualists. Its focus is Storsjön (Great Lake), which is also Sweden's Loch Ness, for the myth about an aquatic monster has been perpetuated for centuries. Jämtland's highlands toward the mountains on the Norwegian boundary include the most widely known regions for winter sports in Sweden. Åre and Storlien are the centers, favorite haunts of the skiers.

Most travelers would by now undoubtedly believe that they had journeyed quite far to the north, but actually we are only near the middle of Sweden. Somewhat south of Östersund, capital of the province, grow three stately pines which indicate the country's geographical center.

There remains the immense, sparsely populated territory of the upper half of Sweden. *Västerbotten* and *Norrbotten* (West

46

and North Bothnia) are the coastal provinces, named after their location in respect to the Gulf of Bothnia. Nowadays sawmills and other forest industries of great importance are located at the mouths of the rivers in these provinces. Quite large settlements have sprung up where such rivers as the Ume, the Skellefte, and the Pite reach the Gulf. In the farming areas frost-resistant grains yield harvests, the size of which can be explained only on the basis of intensive agricultural research.

One discovery made in Västerbotten has extended the concept of "Sweden's Gold Coast" to the upper reaches of the Gulf of Bothnia: the gold deposits at Boliden which also yield silver, copper, sulphur, and other minerals. Large quantities of arsenic is a by-product here. Recently this dangerous poison has been utilized for the impregnation and preservation of wood. It is also used to shorten the life span of locusts in South Africa and other countries. Curiously enough, the location of the large gold veins at Boliden was indicated by Olaus Magnus, Sweden's last Catholic bishop and a learned historian, on his map, *Carta Marina*, printed 1539 in Rome. With the medieval cartographer's fancy he symbolized the region of his *Mina aurea* with an egg-hatching rooster.

To the west of Västerbotten and Norrbotten lies *Lappland*, home of nomadic Lapps and their reindeer, which in its northern part is also the land of the midnight sun and of the midwinter darkness. This immense province with its towering mountains, extensive bogs, and deep forests extends all the way to the Arctic Circle and far beyond. The interior of the region was not made accessible by modern communications until ten years ago when the Inland Railroad was completed. Over a period of twenty-seven years, this road was gradually advanced through an almost complete wilderness.

The relatively few remaining Lapps—around 6 500—keep a total of about 200 000 reindeer as their principal means of livelihood. So far, Lappland has only two towns, Lycksele, capital of the region, and Kiruna. The latter is a well organized, modern community which has grown up around the tremendous, surface-mined Kirunavaara iron ore mountain. With a population of over 10 000, it is considered the world's largest community north of the Arctic Circle. Within Kiruna's liberally drawn town limits lies Kebnekajse, Sweden's highest mountain (6 965 ft.).

Southeast of Kiruna lies Malmberget, an iron ore mine whose net of electric railways through the galleries is more extensive than London's combined undergrounds. From two mines, whose metal yield is one of the highest found anywhere, about five million tons of ore are extracted annually. Most of this is exported but some is smelted and semifinished at the iron works in Luleå. This plant is owned by the state and is, so far, the only instance of government competition with private enterprise in that industry. The reasons for its establishment were largely social.

A few miles southwest of Malmberget, but still well above the Arctic Circle, the government operates the great hydroelectric plant at Porjus, which is scheduled for further enlargement.

Such a rapid survey of the country as we have just sketched is physically possible in the Age of Flight. This bird's-eye view, now realizable in a modern plane, was foretold and described forty years ago by Sweden's famed Selma Lagerlöf. In a book written for the Swedish children she lets Nils Holgersson, a little Skåne boy turned into a thumbling, travel over the whole country with a flock of wild geese through the spring, summer, and autumn. This book is now available in more than a score of languages and in about thirty-five different translations (English: *The Wonderful Adventures of Nils*). Most of what Nils saw, and we in retracing his flight,

22. Swedish children. Photo by Gösta Lundquist.

23 and 24. Two forest workers from Norrland and a road construction vorker from middle Sweden. Photo by Gösta Lundquist.

25. The policeman is helpful. Photo by I. Lindhe.

26. The head of a scientific institution and his assistant. Photo by Gösta Lundquist.

was undeniably forests, for the tilled soil resembles small oases in a desert of green. But Nils also had the opportunity to observe the fields, the towns, and the industrial communities, as does the airline passenger of today. With this air map of the country in mind, we shall give a résumé of Sweden's economic life in the following chapter. Her fundamental resources in soil, mountains, and forests we have now surveyed.

LANGUAGE AND POPULATION

When the English or American visitor encounters the Swedish place names, the close relation between his own language and that of his hosts readily becomes apparent. Many words are identical in spelling: arm — *arm*, finger — *finger*, hand — *hand*, hare — *hare*, son — *son*; others are close cognates in the two languages, such as crown — *krona*, king — *kung*, sea — *sjö*. Others again have in the course of the centuries, while still cognates, diverged in meaning: time — *timme* (hour), tiding — *tidning* (newspaper), flood — *flod* (river).

The Swedish language has borrowed many words from the English in recent years, largely of a technical or economic nature and in the world of sports and entertainment. Words such as 'strike' have been phonetically modified *(strejk)*, others have been adopted unchanged (lockout, handicap, tank, jeep, game, set, clearing, jitterbug). An interesting loan in the other direction is the word *tungsten* ('heavy stone'), the Swedish name for the element discovered by the brilliant chemist Scheele (shālĕ) in the 1780's, often called wolfram. Another is *smörgåsbord*, frequently abused in spelling, pronunciation, and preparation.

The uniformity in place names and in the language as a whole indicates that the same race has lived in Sweden from the earliest times. On the whole, homogeneity in race, language, and religion is one of Sweden's characteristics. An exception is northern Lappland where Lapp and Finnish elements are clearly traceable in the place names.

In 1948 Sweden had a population of more than 6 800 000, including about 34 000 Finns and 6 500 Lapps, but the number of the latter is steadily decreasing. Sociologists value the fact that Sweden's records of vital statistics are the oldest in the world and have been meticulously kept since the middle of the eighteenth century. These records indicate, for instance, an increase in the average height and improved physical characteristics. The greater number of Swedes are fair, with light hair and blue or bluish-gray eyes, but dark hair and brown eyes are by no means exceptional. Immigrations have from time to time left definite traces in the population.

Especially strong was the German penetration in the Middle Ages and the centuries immediately following. According to a statute from the fourteenth century, not more than one half of the members in the municipal administrations could be Germans. Dutchmen and Walloons, the latter natives of Belgium, were induced to move to Sweden and assist in her economic development, particularly in the iron industry. Their descendants are still in evidence. A few Jews immigrated, beginning mostly when King Gustav III granted them official admission toward the end of the eighteenth century. Scotsmen favored Göteborg when they settled in Sweden. In the seventeenth century some Finns migrated to Värmland and other central Swedish provinces. On the other hand, a Swedish population of about 350 000 still live in Finland. They are the descendants of Swedish colonists to that country and have in a high degree preserved the old Swedish traditions, perhaps with less admixture than anywhere else. In Sweden, however, each foreign influx was fairly rapidly assimilated, and today the homogeneity of the population is quite striking.

The greatest immigration, however, has taken place during the past fifteen years, so disastrous to the rest of Europe. Both the government and individuals readily gave asylum to the victims of modern dictatorships. The number of refugees —aliens with residence permit—at the end of World War II totalled about 135 000, the dominant nationalities being Balts, Danes, and Norwegians. Not included in this total are special groups, such as Finnish children and evacuees. Never in Sweden's history have so many people of widely divergent races and languages crossed her borders. Many of these refugees have found regular occupation and taken up permanent residence. The latest figure (1948) is 88 000.

SWEDEN AT WORK

AGRICULTURE

FORESTRY

IRON AND STEEL

»SWEDISH MODERN»
AND OTHER LIGHT MANUFACTURE

WATER POWER

COMMUNICATIONS

FOREIGN TRADE

MONEY AND BANKING

LABOR IN AGRICULTURE AND INDUSTRY

PUBLIC, PRIVATE, AND COOPERATIVE ENTERPRISE

STANDARD OF LIVING

AGRICULTURE

The inhabitants of a Swedish village, Gammalsvenskby, on the banks of the Dnjepr in the interior of Russia, where their ancestors settled in the eighteenth century, returned to Sweden in 1929. Their first and general impression when they were re-settled on Swedish soil was that it required far harder work than the Russian.

Sweden is not a first-rate agricultural country. Really good soil is found only in relatively small and scattered areas; as a rule the soil is rather poor. But in spite of its northern latitude, the country is favored with an exceptionally mild climate because of the Gulf Stream's propitious influence. Somewhat distressing is the tendency toward drought and precipitation at times disadvantageous to the crops. The rains are ordinarily most frequent at harvest time in the late summer.

Swedish agriculture has, nevertheless, reached a high level. The average yield of wheat and sugar beets on the plains of Skåne easily bears comparison with the best agricultural regions anywhere. Sweden's average wheat yield per unit area is surpassed in Denmark, Holland, and Belgium, more than twice as large in the United States, Canada, Argentina, and Australia, but approximately equals that of Switzerland, the United

Kingdom, New Zealand, and Germany. The average yield of sugar beets is higher only in Denmark and Holland.

During normal times Sweden is by and large self-supporting in respect to agricultural products. However, in order to maintain a production adequate for the country, the Swedish farmer depends to a certain extent on the import of artificial fertilizer and feed concentrates. This was, of course, clearly demonstrated during the war. It has been estimated that imported fertilizer and feed account for about 15 % of the total yield. Normally only somewhat more than 10 % of Sweden's import is food, and of this a large share is claimed for coffee, cocoa, fresh fruit, tobacco, and the like.

When Sweden became isolated from the rest of the world during the second world war, the food situation was one of her many precarious problems. Largely because of intensive research, Swedish farmers were able to provide food for the population, though at times the outcome seemed in doubt. It was even possible to furnish some relief to the nation's distressed neighbours. Bread, sugar, meat, and butter were streched into adequacy by strict rationing, a step not necessary for milk. Shortage of lard prompted large-scale cultivation of plants yielding vegetable oil.

While the yield statistics quoted above are quite favorable, the figures on the available arable land tell a different story. About 9 % of Sweden's soil is under cultivation while the British Isles have about 20 %, France 40 %, and Denmark 60 %. These figures should be viewed against the fact that such a large part of Sweden is forest land or mountainous terrain, especially in Norrland. But even there the harvests are good. To be sure, the summer is short, but during the season the crops are exposed to rather intensive sunlight almost around the clock. The three administrative districts farthest north,

60

27. During the nineteenth century the so-called "great redistribution" of land holdings (*storskiftet*) was carried through in large parts of Sweden, which, for one thing, led to the dissolution of the old village system with its partly collectivized agriculture. Some features of the old system still persist. Photo by Gösta Lundquist.

28 and 29. In southern Sweden, especially in Skåne, the country's most important agricultural districts are located. Large-scale experimental research is conducted here at such institutes as Svalöv and Weibulls-holm. Among the results are the hardier grains developed for climatically less favored parts of the country. Left: A Swedish scientist at the Svalöv Agricultural Institute scrutinizes a hardy variety of clover. Photos by Gunnar M. Lager and K. W. Gullers.

30. Farm on the Scanian plain. Photo by Gösta Lundquist.

31 and 32. All the way up to the Arctic Circle, and even beyond it, the soil is cultivated in the northern mountain valleys, mostly for fodder plants and potatoes. A cultivated region in Lappland. Left: Ammarnäs, where the potatoes grown on a frostfree hillock meet the needs of the entire village in respect to this important item on the Swedish menu. Photos by Gösta Lundquist.

33. The Norrland mountain farmers are a hardy and active lot. They work their farms but also fell trees and transport the logs out of the forest. Farmers at Ammarnäs, Lappland, in a story-telling mood. Photos by Gösta Lundquist.

34, 35 and 36. Much of Sweden's economic life is based on the resources of the forests. In the winter the timber is felled and brought out to the river's edge (top of opposite page); during the spring and summer it is floated down to the industrial plants at the shore. Above is the Ljunga River, which carries a large part of the raw material to the forest industries in the Sundsvall district. Lower picture, opposite page: A charcoal kiln in Småland. Photos by Bertil Ekholz, K. W. Gullers and Aeromateriel.

37 and 38. Cellulose processing is Sweden's chief export industry, concentrated on the Norrland coast and in central Sweden. Svartvik in the Sundsvall region, one of the Cellulose Company's plants; left is an interior from a sulfite factory in Värmland, belonging to the Billerud Company.

for instance, show the highest potato yield per acre in the whole country.

Three compensations have been found for the niggardliness of nature: hard work, expert soil chemistry, and successful plant breeding. Nowadays the hard work is somewhat eased by modern farm machinery, much of which was first introduced to the people at home by emigrants returned from the United States. The stone fences that surround so many of the Swedish fields are mute witnesses to the amount of labor expended in clearing the ground before the age of tractors. The scientific knowledge of soils and crops has been furthered by intensive education directed chiefly from the schools of agriculture. An instance of progressive plant breeding is the estimated 30 % increase in the yield of autumn wheat. It has been estimated that plant improvement research adds an annual increment of $ 28 million to farm incomes. Technical training and education have also contributed to the improvement of agriculture.

The institutes at Svalöv, Weibullsholm, and Ultuna are the centers of research and study; professor Herman Nilsson-Ehle is one of Sweden's foremost experts in this important field.

The food supply has also increased as a result of the rationalization to which Swedish agriculture has been subjected in recent years. The farmers have organized into large economic associations, which on a cooperative basis manage dairies, abattoirs, and other enterprises. The oldest of these associations date back to the 1880's. However, they did not really hit their stride until the 1930's, when the international crisis in agriculture made governmental measures to aid the farmers necessary. Far-reaching state controls of prices and conditions for the sale of agricultural products were introduced, which in turn brought about extensive organization work carried on with the help of state subsidies. This development was further accelerated by the fact that the farmers themselves in their precarious position realized the need for united efforts. At present practically every Swedish farmer is a member of one or more of these associations. About 95 % of all milk and butter sales are handled by the dairy associations, and the majority of all deals involving animals to be slaughtered go through the farmer's own organization. To a large extent these also purchase the supplies needed by the farmers, and even procure some of the tractors and other agricultural machinery.

Mechanized farming demands areas much larger than the fenced in and ditched patches still common and intensively cultivated with rotation of crops. But the fences are coming down and the ditches laid with drainage tile, then covered. By now such drainage has been installed in more than one fourth of the acreage under cultivation. An important factor encouraging mechanization is the scarcity of farm labor. 60 % of the farmers' own acreage are too small or otherwise unsuitable for the use of tractor-drawn machinery; consequently, they are dependent on man power. Since as much as 77 % of the farms have less than 25 acres, the new agricultural policy calls for the combining of small holdings to make possible the use of machine implements. Such an arrangement would enable the individual farmer to retain his cherished independence while reaping the advantages of large-scale farming and labor-saving, modern machinery.

Farming and cattle raising are always combined in Sweden; the average farm has five cows. During the war years, fodder conservation became imperative. The solution was siloing, formerly rare in Sweden, and by 1944 an impressive number of silos (23 000) had been constructed.

The conditions under which the farm laborers lived and worked have long been a matter of concern. Their situation has recently been much improved by legislation and other measures; the unsatisfactory tenant farmer system has been entirely eliminated. Efforts are also being made to better the lot of the industrious but poor farmers with insufficient acreage. Many of them are far from adequately rewarded for the amount of labor expended, and different methods to increase small farm efficiency are being tried.

FORESTRY

The statement frequently encountered that Sweden is a land of forests is quite as accurate as formerly. During the war years, however, cutting was necessary to such an extent that the stands were somewhat reduced. The latest survey of the crown forests in central Norrland indicates that the cutting must be reduced to about 60 % of the present rate to prevent a threatening over-thinning, especially of trees felled for heavy timber. Clearly the severe cutting during the war was caused by Sweden's lack of coal, but it is equally obvious that the country cannot afford to cut in excess of the yearly growth. Thus even Sweden is faced with the necessity of reducing the consumption of her forest resources. It is more profitable to use the forests as a source of raw material than for fuel.

The forests have always given Sweden "food and clothing, house and home," to use Martin Luther's phrase. This was truer than ever during the war years. The cattle consumed fodder produced from cellulose by chemical processes. When the motor fuel imports were cut off, the vehicles kept rolling on gas generated from wood or charcoal as they went along. Wall board and alcohol, glue and plastics, clothing and food, a host of other products, all have been conjured out of the

71

forests by the wizardry of science. The United States has blazed new trails in such research, and Sweden strives to keep in step and contribute to further developments. For instance, prefabricated frame houses and auxiliary buildings are today in great demand and have proved a blessing in several of the countries ravaged by the war.

Much lumber is produced in Värmland, Dalarna, and other places in central Sweden, but by far the greater part of the exports comes from Norrland. The demand for lumber and pulp has risen constantly in the world markets during the past hundred years. Sweden has improved the methods of regeneration, handling, and processing. A network of rivers, channels, and chutes has been developed for floating the logs down to the shore. The endless stream of timber is absorbed by the huge saw mills and pulp factories near the river mouths and prepared for export in a variety of semifinished or finished products. Actually the wood industry in its various aspects accounts for almost one seventh of Sweden's total production. Before World War II, about 40 % of the exports by value consisted of forest products. Pulp and paper were the most important items, 70 % of the former and 60 % of the latter being exported. Sweden is the world's largest exporter of pulp and is surpassed only by the United States and Canada in production. The annual value of exported forest products amounted before the war (1939) to somewhat more than 196 million dollars.

Progress must, however, be made in the direction of more effective utilization of the raw material and toward a greater proportion of finished goods and more refined products. Originally the resources of the Swedish forests furnished the basis for the export of timber, and later the pulp industry was developed. Perhaps the future points toward the chemical industry, and intensive research is being carried on in the laboratories. Selective plant breeding brought greatly increased values to farming, and along similar lines attempts are now being made to improve the quality of the forests. The slow growth has traditionally made Swedish timber an excellent raw material. But the supply is not inexhaustible, and rationalization is necessary. Since the forests industries are very sensitive to fluctuations in the business cycle, compensatory measures must be found, such as new ways of utilizing the available man power.

The hard work involved in logging puts its stamp on the people's life in the forest regions during the winter; driving the logs down the streams in spring and summer lends color and activity to those seasons. The working conditions of the lumberman have long constituted a serious social problem, but they have in recent years been considerably improved. Well constructed, temporary barracks are used more and more extensively, and in many places women cooks have been engaged to ensure better meals and a more proper diet. Efforts are continued to raise the standards of the lumber camps still further and make the life of the workers more agreeable during the long periods they are away from their homes.

At present, municipal and state ownership accounts for one fourth of the forests, companies own another fourth, and individuals, mostly farmers, the remaining half. When the extensive exploitation of forest resources began, it was feared that the companies would in one way or another gain possession of too large a part of the privately owned stands. Soon after the turn of the century parliament took action and by legal measures secured the farmers' share. Since the state normally draws an annual net profit of 6—7 million dollars from its forests, conservation is also a matter of national concern, and intensive research dealing with the regeneration of forests is carried on. Obvious difficulties are inherent in this study; after all, it takes a generation before the results of some experiments can be obtained.

The wealth of the forests—and of mineral deposits—is not without its problems in the far north. Efforts are made to overcome the disadvantages caused by the location and climate, efforts which still are in their early stages. For instance, compensatory measures are sought to diminish the drawbacks resulting from the isolation in widely scattered and sparsely populated settlements. More rapid and frequent communications, better educational opportunities, extended vocational training, and cheaper freight rates are some of the steps taken or planned for the benefit of those who live in this vast and rugged region.

IRON AND STEEL

In Nature's bounty to Sweden the produce of the fields and the timber of the forests are complemented by the ore from mountains and mines. This plenteous gift is found principally throughout the metal belt across central Sweden and farthest up in Norrland. Iron ore also exists in Skåne but has not yet been mined.

Unfortunately, fossil fuel deposits do not coexist in Sweden with those of ore. The nearest solution to the fuel problem would seem to be the use of pure but expensive charcoal or the importation of anthracite. But instead, because of the difference in shipping costs, the phosphoreted ore is exported to countries rich in coal, mainly England and Germany, but nowadays also to the United States. This is all the more practical because of the high quality of the ore; the iron content of the Kiruna mine runs up to 70 %, higher than that of any other known deposit. The iron ore of Bergslagen is of lower content but unusually free from sulphur and phosphorus, making it especially suitable for the manufacture at home of high-grade iron and steel. Iron has, of course, always played an important role in Sweden's economy. In the seventeenth and eighteenth centuries she was the greatest producer in the world of this basic metal and was surpassed only when England discovered ways of using fossil coal for the smelting and processing. Sweden today not only manufactures but also imports considerable quantities of commercial iron.

Before the war more than eight million tons of ore were extracted annually, an amount surpassed only by the United States, Russia, Germany, and France. Annual exports have run as high as fifteen million metric tons (1937), stock piles accumulated at some mines during low export years in the early 30's accounting for the quantity beyond annual production. Close to 65 million dollars worth of ore was shipped abroad in 1939.

About a million tons of ore are processed each year by the native iron and steel industries. In one of Esaias Tegnér's lines, the famous Swedish poet praises "the edge of Swedish steel." While he related the phrase to earlier, warlike exploits, the phrase applies equally well to the many peaceful products whose Swedish origin is a guarantee of quality all over the world, such as knives, razor blades, and saws.

At one time Sweden was primarily an agricultural country. Today industry and manufacture support 2.5 million people, while only 1.9 million derive their livelihood from the soil. The percentage of population engaged in industry is higher only in Switzerland, Belgium, the Netherlands, Germany, and the United Kingdom. This development is chiefly due to three factors: the quality of the raw material, high technical skill, and the contributions of Swedish inventors on which ten percent of the country's industries are based. The inventions, in turn, often depend on the quality of the native steel. C. E. ("Precision") Johansson, for instance, during several decades one of Henry Ford's closest and highest paid associates, based his ingenious slip gauges, the precision blocks, on a special Swedish steel. The same is true of Sven Wingquist's ball bearings, an invention which developed into a world industry. Swedish ball bearings were in such demand during the last war that quantities of them were fetched by daring blockade runners in English motor torpedo boats from Swedish west coast ports for the factories of the Allies. Perhaps the deliveries were agreed upon over L. M. Ericsson's telephones; the little speedboats may have been built in one of the Göteborg yards, such as the Göta Works, Sweden's largest shipbuilder, Eriksberg, or Lindholmen, or at the Kockum Shipyards in Malmö. On a peace-time run they would probably have been guided by the automatic beacons invented by the Nobel Prize winner, Gustaf Dalén. The great AGA Works exploit primarily the inventions by Dalén, such as his famous sun valve. ASEA, Sweden's General Electric Company, bases much of its production on the discoveries of Josef Wenström relative to the transmission of electric power. While every farmhand knows that a separator extracts the cream from the whole milk, few people would know that the inventor, Gustaf de Laval, was a Swede who also played an important part in the development of steam turbines. A number of industries have sprung from the inventions of the Ljungström brothers, especially in the field of steam engineering.

During the war the metal industries were largely converted to the manufacture of defense matériel. But the Bofors guns had attracted the attention of foreign ordnance departments before that and played a significant part in the Battle of Britain as early as 1940. Bofors was formerly owned by Alfred

39. Papermaking machine. Photo by Inge Holm.

40. The quest for ore goes on uninterruptedly. Considerable finds have been made in the vast regions of Lappland during the past decade with the aid of electrical detectors, while mining of course continues in the fields already being exploited. Photo Boliden.

41 and 42. Above: Kiruna in the light of an arctic evening. Photo by Carl Holm.
Below: Surface mining at the famous Boliden mine in Västerbotten. Photo Boliden.

43. Interior from a Bofors foundry in Värmland. Bofors enjoys an international reputation, especially because of its important production of war materiel. Photo by Bofors.

44 and 45. The good repute of Swedish iron and steel is traditional. Nowadays the iron industry in Sweden is primarily engaged in making quality goods for export. One of the prime factors in this work is an important Swedish invention, C. E. ("Precision") Johansson's gauge blocks, shown here. Above: Inspection of steel bands at the Hagfors Works, a plant belonging to the Uddeholm Company. Photos by Lennart af Petersens and the Technological Museum.

46. Göteborg is the center of the Swedish shipbuilding industry. The three large ship-yards of Eriksberg, Göta Works, and Lindholmen account for a considerable share of the tonnage built in Sweden. Interior from the Göta Works. Photo by K. W. Gullers.

47. Sweden has many important concerns in the electrical industry. Best known internationally are the L. M. Ericsson Company and ASEA, the former for its telephones, the latter for such products as generators and transformers. Photo by K. W. Gullers.

48. Swedish ball bearings, famed throughout the world, are an excellent example of a Swedish quality goods industry. Photo by K. W. Gullers.

Nobel and continues to exploit his inventions and discoveries; the gunpowder manufactured there is named after him. In line with the people's ready acceptance of scientific progress, various groups, particularly in industry, early became airminded, and Sweden today possesses a growing aircraft industry. One of the latest of its products is a fast pushpropeller pursuit plane, now being redesigned for jet propulsion. A sports plane of Swedish manufacture and flown by a Swedish pilot established a world long distance record on a flight to Ethiopia in May, 1947. The Swedish automobile industry made an early start and has been especially successful in developing truck and bus models which compare favorably with America's best.

The swift conversion of the metal industries into defense plants when the war broke out in 1939 has been matched by a smooth reconversion to peacetime production. For example, the great armament works at Bofors, which recently were immersed in ordnance manufacture, now are also engaged in the manufacture of certain medicinal products.

"SWEDISH MODERN" AND OTHER LIGHT MANUFACTURE

Most visitors to world fairs and other general expositions have probably at one time or another examined a representative display of contemporary Swedish arts and crafts. The Swedish manner in the decorative arts, although the products cannot be said to have any particular characteristic in common, has been given the collective name of "Swedish Modern." Most popular and familiar is the graceful, carefully designed and executed glassware, leading producers of which are the glassworks at

85

Orrefors and Kosta. The war years called for "sterner stuff" on the world markets, but with the cessation of hostilities many of these delicate products have again come into demand.

Less international in nature are the numerous and varied industries producing for home consumption, many of which work with imported raw materials. In this group belong the extensive textile, knitted goods, and clothing industries, as well as the manufacturers of rubber goods, shoes, furnitures, and porcelain. Here should also be mentioned the versatile small-scale, or shop industry, since it is indicative of the people's talent for technical work and mechanics. Foremost in such activity is the province of Småland, but progress along this line is also rapid in Norrland. One observer traveling in the northern parts recently told of a village where he had found no less than thirty-five separate little factories. In a Småland community, for example, one man makes an almond grinder, another snap fasteners, a third heelplates, a fourth wooden rake pegs, etc. Not infrequently, an automatic and personally invented machine carries on while the "manufacturer" works his farm or enjoys his afternoon coffee. Manufacturers' associations are established in the various districts and extend loans at low interest to further the development of the small-scale industries. These associations receive grants from the government, this being one of the ways in which enterprise is encouraged, especially in the regions where the economic life is too one-sided.

WATER POWER

During the blockade of the last war Sweden's lack of coal caused a serious fuel problem. The small deposits in Skåne are normally used to fill local requirements, most of the coal being consumed by the ceramic works at Höganäs in the north-west of the province. Charcoal is expensive to prepare, and the iron industry holds priority on the amount produced.

Fortunately the exploitation of water power has made great strides since the turn of the century. During recent decades, electrification has proceeded so rapidly that, for instance, three-fourths of the Swedish farms now have electricity. The utilization of the water falls and rapids as energy producers is in constant progress and will be complete within the next few decades. New construction and enlargements of existing plants are now under way on a generous scale. Nine percent of Sweden's area is composed of lakes and rivers, the latter generally flowing from north to south, as has already been indicated. While the falls, as a rule, are not large, heavy and dependable drainage from the lakes makes practical the construction of sizable dams to obtain a satisfactory level.

Exploitable water power is estimated at about 8 000 000 kilowatts, of which only about one-third has been utilized so far. But the annual output of the hydroelectric plants, which in 1913 was about 1.5 billion kilowatt hours, now amounts to approximately 14 billion kilowatt hours, or almost nine times the consumption just before World War I. Even if the exploitable water power were utilized to the full, it would make possible a maximum consumption of only 36 billion kilowatt hours. Import of oil and other fuel will always be necessary. A shortage entailing temporary rationing of electric power from time to time is therefore experienced.

The largest hydroelectric plant is Trollhättan, located about fifty miles north of Göteborg. Appropriately enough, the country's largest lake, Vänern, serves as the natural reservoir of the plant. During the summer, consumption is controlled so as to economize on and store up the water of the lake. The water supply in the Norrland rivers is relatively low in winter, and the huge plant at Trollhättan acts as a reserve supply for the north country.

Eighty percent of the total kilowatt reserves are to be found in Norrland. The high capacity plant at Porjus, already mentioned, is located far above the Arctic Circle and for the most part deep under the ground. Not far away is the famous waterfall Harsprånget (Hare's Leap), long a tourist attraction, where another giant hydroelectric plant is now under construction.

The government, some municipalities, and several private companies produce electric energy but work hand in glove on distribution and rates. Of the total energy, the state plants supply 40 %, the municipalities 6 %, and private companies the remaining 54 %. Industrial concerns generating power mostly for their own use account for more than a third of the private company percentage. Transmission lines are coordinated so that each of the larger plants can supply energy to any part of Sweden.

COMMUNICATIONS

When Sweden began building railroads in earnest soon after the middle of the nineteenth century, the guiding principle was that the government was to be responsible for the country's most important railway lines, while the feeder lines were left to private enterprise. By and large this plan has been followed, but for a number of years there has been no new construction of either state or private railways. Meantime, parliament has decreed that the state will gradually take over all private lines. In 1947 the only large line remaining in private ownership was transferred to the state, which now owns about

49. The Norrland rivers with their rapids and falls have been utilized as an important source of power for Swedish industry and communications. Part of Krångede hydroelectric plant on the Indal River. Photo by Gösta Lundquist.

50. The Swedish railways and the communications system as a whole enjoy a good reputation for both safety and comfort. Construction of a high-speed locomotive at the Linköping Works.

51 and 52. International communications are handled by several Swedish companies. In the picture above the Swedish American Line's "Stockholm" leaves the Göteborg harbor for the United States. The other view is from Bromma, the Stockholm airport, from which routes fan out to all parts of the world. Photos by Gösta Lidén and Lennart af Petersens.

53 and 54. A bridge connecting two nations: The Svinesund span between Norway and Sweden. Below: A waterway and tourist route through the country. Locks in the Göta Canal. Photos by Gunvor Ahlberg and J.-E. Andersson.

80 % of the country's total trackage. Furthermore, the State Railways carry a much greater share of the traffic than the percentage indicates, since the private lines are small and not heavily used. Sweden's railroad trackage totals over 10 000 miles, or about 1 $^2/_3$ miles per inhabitant. The latter figure places Sweden fifth in the world as a railroad country, the leaders being Canada, Australia, New Zealand, and the United States. Traffic is heavy and amounts to nearly 1.9 billion passenger miles, about 4.1 billion ton-miles of freight annually. Since the use of steam produced with imported coal has proved too expensive, the electrification of the railroad net has gone on apace. About one-third of the trackage is now electrified, but this third accounts for 85 % of the total traffic, for it includes all of the main lines.

Long before the railroad age, canals played a considerable role in Sweden's communications and are still far from obsolete. The famed Göta Canal, built in the first half of the last century, crosses the country east to west, taking advantage wherever possible of the many lakes and natural waterways. An enthusiastic Englishman once called this remarkable route "the fresh-water path through romance," and the trip through the Canal has practically become a "must" for the foreign visitor. About 50 000 passages are made by ship through the various Swedish canals annually and the lock fees alone amount to about half a million dollars.

The sea lanes are of vital importance to modern Sweden. Since the first world war the merchant fleet has almost doubled and the tonnage today, despite the heavy war loss of about two hundred vessels, is greater than ever before. The ships are among the most modern in the world, the majority of them motor-driven and built on Swedish ways. Before the war Sweden ranked sixth among the shipbuilding nations, but the 1948 figures indicate that only Great Britain builds more at present. The 1947 gross tonnage of 1 907 000 placed Sweden seventh among seafaring nations.

Swedish steamship companies maintain routes to all continents and also engage in much international shipping which does not touch at the home country. Since Sweden carries on such a relatively large foreign trade, shipping obviously plays a major role in her economy. More than 90 % of that trade is carried by water, and of this percentage one half in Swedish bottoms. Shipping income for 1947 was estimated at 160 million dollars—an important item in the Swedish balance of trade.

The domestic air lines have developed rapidly and the regular routes now include the upper regions of Norrland, where as many as twenty-five years ago ambulance planes performed rescues which attracted international attention. A trip from one end of the country to the other is now possible and saves the traveler two entire days, as compared with the same journey by train. Large air fields are under construction to meet the demands of the increasing international traffic. On the intercontinental routes the Swedish lines cooperate with the other Scandinavian countries.

FOREIGN TRADE

Sweden maintains commercial relations with almost every country in the world. Total exports and imports in 1939 amounted to about 1.2 billion dollars—$1/_{33}$ of the world trade—with an import surplus of about 170 million dollars. In 1947 the "adverse" trade balance rose to more than 540 million dollars in round figures. The resulting import surplus reflects the growth of the dollar crisis in Europe during 1947 and indicates the need of the import restrictions Sweden had to put into effect on October 1, 1947. Sweden is at all times eager to sell but appears to be an even better customer.

Forest industry products lead in Swedish exports; lumber, paper, and pulp accounted for 40 % of the total in 1939. In the years before World War II, Sweden was unchallenged as an exporter of both chemical and mechanical pulp, supplying about one-half of the total world export. In paper she was second only to Canada. Ore and metal products made up 35 % of the total exports, placing Sweden second only to France in this classification. Agricultural exports—chiefly butter and live cattle—totalled a mere 10 %. Swedish farming is obviously aimed primarily at the home markets.

Manufactured products rank highest in the imports. Food stuffs for people and animals amount to about 20 % of the imports in normal times: grain, vegetable oils and fats, oil cake, fruit, and colonial produce, including coffee and tobacco. About 15 % is fuel: coal, coke, gasoline, and fuel oils.

The distribution of trade to foreign countries is indicative of the normal connections in time of peace. England was Sweden's best customer and bought 24 % of the total exports, Germany following with 18 %, and the United States with 9 %. Sweden's immediate neighbors, Denmark, Norway, and Finland, bought a combined total of 16 % of the exports.

Trade with the United States and other non-European countries, import as well as export, has increased greatly in the postwar period. The chief imports used to come from Germany—coal, chemicals, iron, and machinery; the United States has now taken her place with cotton, wheat, motor fuel, and machinery.

The difficulties in the foreign trade depend not only upon the fact that Germany has lost her prewar status of being the chief source for Swedish imports. Many other European countries have had their export capacity greatly lowered by the war. Consequently, "hard-currency countries," such as the United States, Switzerland, Portugal, and Latin America, have increased their share in Sweden's import from about one-fourth in the years before the war to about one-half at the present. A similar trend is evident in respect to exports; hard-currency countries now absorb 30 % instead of the former 10 % of the total. Exports to the United States, however, have declined from 11 % of Sweden's total in 1936—1938 to 7 % for 1946.

While Sweden was isolated in Europe during the last war, her foreign trade decreased sharply and amounted to not much more than half of the prewar normal, or about 700 million dollars. In the past two years, 1945—1947, this figure has risen considerably, and the Swedish exporters stand ready to send more and more of their goods to foreign parts. With industry products, machinery, and ore Sweden hopes to continue her contribution toward the task of reconstruction and rehabilitation.

MONEY AND BANKING

When toward the end of the last century Sweden was about to begin building railroads on a large scale, unthinkable without the aid of foreign capital, loans were obtained by the government, chiefly from England, France, and Germany, to finance the construction of the far-flung State Railways. An English firm was at first engaged to construct the ore railway from Luleå to Gällivare when the great ore discoveries were to be exploited, but the Swedes themselves later took over this task.

For major undertakings and emergencies, Sweden was dependent on foreign capital up to the beginning of the twentieth century. Since that time the situation has been reversed and for the past twenty-five years or so the country has been able to export capital. This policy was continued during the first three years after the war, and sizable loans, mostly in the form of commercial credits, were extended to a number of countries. In order to contribute as much as possible toward the reconstruction work in Europe, Sweden granted government credits to her neighbor countries, to Holland, England, and others, mostly her former chief customers, for more than $ 420 million and gifts in excess of $ 250 million in connection with the end of the war and in the period immediately following. The credits in question had been almost completely exhausted by mid-1946. During the actual postwar period Sweden has extended credits for about $ 336 million. Included in this sum are well over $ 280 million granted to Russia in connection with a five-year credit and trade agreement, through which Russia will in part replace Germany as one of Sweden's export-import partners. The annual credits to Russia are to amount to about 56 million dollars, but the exports to the Soviet Union probably will not amount to even 10 % of Sweden's total sales to foreign countries.

Together with many other European countries, though to a less degree, Sweden is at present in the throes of the dollar crisis. Formerly the surplus gained from exports to the Continent could be used for purchases in the United States, and thus a balance was struck. Now efforts must be directed toward a separate export-import balance with the United States.

The Swedish money unit is the *krona* (Engl. 'crown'), plural *kronor;* there are 100 *öre* to the *krona*. The exchange rates for the English pound and the American dollar remained nearly constant for a period of years, but the value of the *krona* was deliberately appreciated by 16.7 % in 1946. A pound is now equivalent to Kr. 14.47, and a dollar Kr. 3.60. The change was one of the steps in the government's efforts to prevent inflation, a danger also held back by a system of careful price control.

Swedish banking has a long and interesting history. Unlike the United States, for example, Sweden has only one central bank of issue. The *Riksbank,* or Bank of Sweden, has been owned by the state since 1668 and was the first occidental bank to issue paper money. Control of the Bank is vested in the *Riksdag* (Parliament), but under the democratic system the Government and the Bank naturally work together in respect to economic policies. Thus one of the chief duties of the Bank is to assist the government authorities in shaping the exchange and currency policies of the country. Its actual business activity is on a very small scale, and the direct contact with the public is limited to such matters as housing and scholarship loans, which, by the way, play an important role in Sweden. Surplus funds of the commercial banks are carried by the Bank of Sweden in checking accounts, on which no interest is paid. In case of temporary shortage of liquid funds, the private banks may obtain credit in the Bank of Sweden through various methods, such as the rediscounting of commercial papers or by furnishing collaterals. The Bank of Sweden has branch offices in all provincial capitals and in some other towns.

The commercial, privately owned banks were started early in the last century. The number of banks, at one time quite large, has gradually been decreased by mergers, and today twenty-two remain. Of these, only a few are influential and maintain branches throughout the country. All in all, there are about a thousand banks and branch offices in Sweden. In 1947 the commercial banks declared assets of nearly 2.8 billion dollars. Paper money in circulation during the same year

98

totalled about 2.9 billion crowns, equivalent to about 784 million dollars.

In addition to the commercial banks Sweden has 460 savings banks, of which at least one is found in every community of any size. They report more than 4 $^1/_2$ million pass-books issued, indicating that almost two-thirds of the population have savings accounts. These banks date back to 1820; their deposits are used largely for local credit needs, especially home-loan financing. Their total deposits were over 6.5 billion crowns, or about 1.8 billion dollars, in 1947. Postal savings are also popular, and the post office department reports about 4.2 million accounts. The insurance companies are, of course, also essentially savings institutions. The life insurance policies in Sweden number more than four millions with a total face value of more than eight billion crowns, or almost two billion dollars.

LABOR IN AGRICULTURE AND INDUSTRY

The ways and means for getting the nation's work done have undergone considerable changes through the ages. In agriculture, communal efforts have been utilized, either wholly or in part, from about 500 A.D. until fairly recently, without at any time representing collectivism in the modern sense. However, more and more of the communal land came into private possession, more and more of the work was done independently by the individual farmer, and in modern times only an occasional area of grazing land remained common village property. Various circumstances had also contributed to the division of the private plots into smaller and smaller strips. In the beginning of the 19th century it was found necessary to pass the so-called Enclosure Act which, in due course, dissolved the old village communities and enabled each farmer to exchange his small, scattered parcels for one or more sizable tracts. This was the prerequisite for modern farming. But today's tractors and other modern machinery make new demands both on the farmer's budget and his acreage. As indicated previously, fences and ditches are removed to make this machinery more practical; the economic organizations of the farmers point in the same direction. This time, however, the combining of efforts is voluntary and cooperative rather than inherited and communal.

Cooperation in the farming communities involves not only large-scale purchase of needed supplies and sale of farm products, but also the acquisition and shared use of larger agricultural machinery, such as heavy tractors, threshing machines, etc. Much remains to be done to modernize the Swedish farms; in many regions this is especially true in regard to piped water, proper sewerage, and other sanitary facilities. The process of bringing the work methods on the farms truly up to date is also far from completed. The new departure in agricultural policy toward establishing larger and more economical cultivation units has already been mentioned.

Swedish industry and its methods have perhaps made more impressive general progress than the farms, especially in production, packaging, and marketing of goods. Industry's major problem has been the labor-management relations. The workers by no means reached their goals without opposition but gradually achieved recognition of their right to organize and to establish wages by collective bargaining. In 1898 the industrial workers formed the Confederation of Swedish Trade Unions, *Landsorganisationen*, commonly abbreviated to LO. In the early years of the labor struggle the strike was a frequently employed weapon.

The success of the unions is reflected not only in the membership of 1 211 000—in a population of 6.8 millions—but also in the wages attained. Between 1860 and 1905 the pay of a qualified industrial worker doubled; since then it has, of course, increased further. In the period 1913—1945 a lumberman's wage almost tripled. Hours and working conditions have been subject to corresponding improvements.

The formation of LO led to a similar step on the part of the employers. In 1902 the Swedish Employers' Confederation, *Svenska Arbetsgivareföreningen,* was founded for the purpose of creating a common front against the strikes. As in other countries the lockout was the principal weapon employed by management.

A test of strength was not long in coming. Seven years later the pressure of an economic world crisis brought about a nation-wide general strike which became the most bitter labor-management struggle ever fought in Sweden.

This conflict caused a temporary decline in the union movement, and by and large the labor market was quiet until the early 1920's. To be sure, there were local strikes during the first world war, caused by discrepancies between wages and the cost of living. The postwar period after 1918 was relatively unsettled, and it was only in the years preceding World War II that the labor situation was truly stabilized. During the recent war both management and labor were eager to avoid open conflicts. Near the end of the European war, however, there was a shift in attitude, mostly because of declining real wages, and in the first half of 1945 a strike occured in the metal industries. This was the greatest conflict since the general strike in 1909 and even surpassed the latter in terms of lost working days (11 300 000), but of course not in importance.

Both labor and management have increasingly turned to peaceful means of reaching agreements, even though mutual suspicion was rather strong at first. A significant innovation was the injection of government conciliators into serious labor

101

disputes as early as 1906. Either labor or management, or both, may call for the service of such a mediator in a dispute, or the mediator may take the initiative, if a breakdown in the negotiations threatens the common interest and public good. It should be remembered, however, that this process is one of mediation, not arbitration, and a conciliator makes no awards or binding decisions. Most of the negotiations are successfully concluded by the parties themselves.

An important forward step was the Law of Collective Bargaining passed in 1928. This law also established a Labor Court, two members of which represent the employers, two labor, two are lawyers, and the seventh an impartial expert; a representative of the employees also participates in the Labor Court in connection with problems relating to his area. All are appointed by the King in Council. The unions were opposed to the Court at first but are by now in favor of it. Differences over the interpretation of a contract, or charges that a contract has been broken, cannot be made the basis for a strike or a lockout. They must be brought before the Labor Court, whose decision is binding and final. An employer violating a contract by an attempt, say, to increase working hours, a union calling a "wildcat" strike, or even the violation by an individual employee is liable for damages. The court, the unions, and management have jointly developed significant techniques and precedents in the field of labor law. The successful operation of the Labor Court has partly prompted the statement that Swedish practices "deserve the most careful study by American observers."

An important distinction between the government conciliators and the Labor Court should be borne in mind. The former deal only with disputes relating to negotiations for a new contract, while the Court deals with differences arising from contracts already signed and in effect.

A leading characteristic of labor-management relations to-day is the extent to which they are governed by collective agreements. By 1943 some 15 000 contracts were in force which fixed wages, piece-work rates, and other conditions for about 1 200 000 workers, i. e. practically all of Sweden's industrial labor. Even the few segments of industry not directly regulated by such agreements generally follow their standards. Thus almost all of Sweden's industry is covered by terms arrived at in collective bargaining and set down in collective agreements. Moreover, eighty percent of the agreements are nation-wide in scope. A single agreement, for example, covers the terms of employment for the metal industry of the whole nation. Obviously such a national scale of bargaining has the advantage of ensuring the stability of an entire industry during the life of a contract; the corresponding disadvantage is that a conflict involving the contract also becomes national.

Part of the credit for the generally smooth operation of Swedish labor-management relations is ascribable to the safe-guards and regulations written into the nation's law. Many aspects of working conditions, safety measures, social welfare, basic working hours, and the like are included in the legal provisions and thus removed from the scope of bargaining. The right to organize and the obligation of either party to enter into negotiations when so requested by the other are examples of principles long recognized, but they were officially included in a law passed in 1936.

But self-regulatory and cooperative efforts characterize the Swedish labor situation even more than the legal features and have given it a reputation for peaceful settlements and stability. Foreign observers have often spoken of an "ability to get along" and a "sense of community responsibility" on the part of both management and labor. Both have made it an avowed objective to handle their own affairs as much as possible and minimize the need for governmental action and regulation. With this in mind both parties met in conference at Saltsjöbaden, a seaside resort near Stockholm, in 1938. The far-reaching discussions carried on there resulted in an epochal agreement on the self-regulation of disputes, the basic principles needed to prevent unnecessary conflicts, and provisions to protect the interests of third parties. A special board for the arbitration of certain types of disagreements was also created. This document and its later supplements and amendments have become widely known as the "Saltsjöbaden agreements." The atmosphere of compromise and understanding which prevailed during these deliberations has enriched the Swedish language with the phrase "the Saltsjöbaden spirit."

Soon after the outbreak of World War II the LO and the employers' association arrived at a flexible agreement based on the cost of living index, the Index Wage Agreement. Incidentally, this method spread beyond the organized workers and soon applied to practically all wage earners. But even this development did not entirely prevent frictions. The extensive strike by the metal workers referred to above was the first one of importance in a long time. Since the spring of 1945 important negotiations about new agreements affecting large parts of the labor market have taken place. In 1946 labor-management settled 99.9 % of all negotiations peacefully. Only 26 000 working days were lost that year because of strikes, a record low. Both sides seem to make every effort to avoid conflicts.

After the first world war Sweden was troubled by a serious unemployment problem. Early in 1933 the unemployed numbered over 185 000. A special government agency, now known as the Royal Labor Board, was established to deal with the problem. Meantime the situation has reversed itself, and the present problem is to procure man power rather than work.

Unemployment was practically nonexistent during the war years. The fears that it may reoccur have not yet materialized. In an attempt to forestall a threatening depression, plans have been made for financial flexibility and expansion.

In 1945 Sweden's industries employed 640 000 workers, of whom 20 % were women. Factories are found in every part of the country, and there are no districts of industrial concentration comparable to those in England, Germany, and the United States. New industries have sprung up where old ones have been discontinued, partly on the basis of certain local advantages but also because of the available man power. Formerly the proximity to iron resources or water power played an important role. Many of the workers nowadays own their own homes, and no friction or real contrast exists between rural and town districts.

Swedish concerns are on the whole quite small. In the approximate total of 22 000 only 10 % employ more than fifty workers. There are only 170 establishments with more than 500 employees. These last concerns engage a scant third of the total number of workers.

Some of the best and most promising aspects of modern Sweden are found in a new type of industrial community which has been developed. Many large concerns have taken an exemplary interest in the living conditions of their workers, and this attitude is gaining ground in other areas as well.

The question of an "industrial democracy" is a notable phase of public opinion and debate at present. The moot point is to what extent the workers should share in the information about the status of the concern which employs them and participate in its management. Obviously opinions on this matter are widely divergent, but positive results leading to increased cooperation between labor and management have already been achieved.

PUBLIC, PRIVATE, AND COOPERATIVE ENTERPRISE

The part played by the state in Sweden's economic life is considerable. Government participation in business did not have to wait for the labor party's coming into power; the start had been made and the precedent established long before that. The state owns and operates most of the railroad trackage; its post office depàrtment not only handles the mails but also operates a savings bank and a checking account service. The public telegraph and telephone networks are managed economically and efficiently by the government. More than a third of the electrical energy is generated in state plants. The state is part owner in certain mines, particularly the important ore deposits in upper Norrland. Parts of the forest industry are operated by the government in connection with the extensive state forests. Up to the present the government has entered industry largely for "social" reasons. It has stepped in where an industry would otherwise have been discontinued and caused unemployment in its region, or it has erected establishments, such as the iron and steel plant in Luleå, to improve the opportunities for employment.

Several monopolies of a semi-governmental nature have been established. All tobacco goods and liquor are marketed and to a great extent manufactured by monopoly companies in which the government dominates. A nationwide restaurant chain, SARA, now exists as a branch company of the liquor monopoly. The profits from the state lottery are used for the support of various cultural projects. Farm subsidies led to a semigovernmental monopoly in the grain imports. Radio broadcasting is a semiofficial monopoly in the form of a company with the Press and the Radio Industry as share holders. The government appoints four of the seven regular members of the board. Each radio owner pays an annual fee of 3.00 dollars. Even the soccer pools are under government direction.

Thus the state is extensively engaged in business and so far mostly in what may be called "public utilities." This tendency increased during the war when the government had to extend such activities to other important fields. The necessary controls imposed on the food and fuel supplies were a government responsibility and involved extensive purchases and redistribution. Likewise the government was faced with the task of procuring raw materials for industry in general and for a good part of the defense industry necessitated by the war-induced military reorganization.

An important part of the general economic discussions revolves about the question whether the government should continue its economic expansion. The answer requires an acquaintance with the role played by private and cooperative enterprise in modern Sweden. It should be evident from the preceding descriptions of various phases of the country's economic life that private enterprise still produces all but a small part of the total goods. Actually, private manufacturing industry is responsible for 95 % of Sweden's production, the cooperatives a mere 4 %, and the government only 1 %. Free competition with its attendant advantages is in all fairness recognized and valued even by those who advocate further business ventures on the part of the state. Thus the pro or con attitude toward a "planned economy" is vital in the current political debate, but circumstances alter cases so much that even those whose general principles place them in the "con" camp prefer to decide each case on its own merits.

Side by side with private and public enterprise the cooperatives make a significant contribution to the economic life of the nation. The Cooperative Association, *Kooperativa För-*

bundet, abbr. KF, was founded in 1899; a recent statement reports 7 300 retail stores and almost 900 000 members, the latter representing a third of the country's households. The retail trade remains the major activity of the consumer cooperatives and their turnover constitutes 14 % of Sweden's total. They specialize in food retailing and sell 20—25 % of all groceries bought by the consumers.

KF also operates flour mills and owns plants manufacturing margarine, shoes, rubbers, galoshes, and light bulbs. As indicated above, cooperative production is not extensive but exerts a decisive influence on prices and quality of the goods just mentioned. In accordance with its constitution, the KF is neutral in respect to religion and politics. In its membership all groups of society are represented, but manual labor is quite definitely dominant. The cooperative movement has always been closely identified with the labor unions, and the latters' success in Sweden also advanced the cause of the cooperatives. However, in recent years KF has assumed a particularly independent position versus the governing Social Democratic Party in the economic debates. Not long ago the cooperatives strongly opposed a government proposal to establish a state oil monopoly as well as a proposed tax revision. KF is also one of the public and private institutions consulted by the government on legislative proposals. The KF management, idealistic and businesslike at the same time, is proceeding according to extensive, long-range plans and have given this movement the strong and recognized position it now holds.

The associations which operate dairies and abattoirs, as well as the purchasing associations which procure artificial fertilizers and seed grain are typical examples of cooperation in agriculture. These producer cooperatives—not to be confused with KF; there is no affiliation—play an important role and constantly gain new adherents. In 1944, for example, the

55 and 56. The Bank of Sweden, first bank in the world to issue paper money, was founded 1668 in Stockholm and is the oldest banking institution still in operation. At top is a Swedish "ten-spot", and below is shown how newly minted one-crown pieces are polished. Photos by Lena Böklin and Bertil Norberg.

57 and 58. A post office and a grocery store in Stockholm. Photos by Bo Törngren and Karl Sandels.

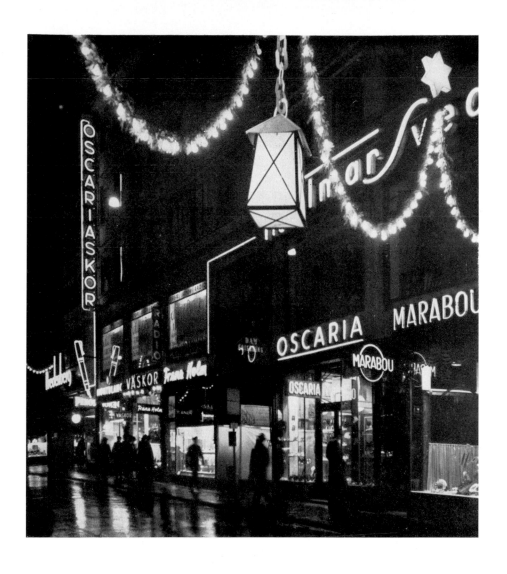

59. Drottninggatan, one of Stockholm's shopping streets, at Christmas time. Photo by Albert Asplund.

60. A normal weekday afternoon on Kungsgatan (King Street), one of Stockholm's main shopping streets. Photo by K. W. Gullers.

cooperative dairies produced, as already mentioned, 95 % of the total dairy products. At the present time the small industries are successfully testing and adopting the cooperative methods used by the farmers.

The municipalities are also in business, primarily in connection with public transportation and utilities, such as tramways, busses, and gasworks. Like the government monopolies, these services are often organized as companies with a certain percentage of private investors and limited dividends. An interesting example of joint action by private industries and a municipality is the Krångede hydroelectric plant, one of the country's largest and located in central Norrland, which is owned by the City of Stockholm and some of the larger industrial concerns.

The interplay of public, private, and cooperative enterprise is among the most characteristic features of Sweden today. The resulting competition stimulates greater efficiency and is a fruitful source for the lively and sometimes heated discussions on private initiative versus additional state ventures in business.

STANDARD OF LIVING

In attempting to determine whether the Swedish standard of living is high, average, or low, a foreign observer would be misled if he tried to judge by his experiences in the capital. While much progress has been made during the past forty years in caring for the unfortunates in Sweden, many peoples are still in straitened or poor circumstances, a fact which neither can nor should be denied.

International statistics compiled before the war indicate that Sweden compares favorably with other countries in most

113

respects. Random items are an average life expectancy greater than elsewhere, except in Holland, Australia, and New Zealand, and an infant mortality rate which is lower only in New Zealand.

The wage statistics also provide some of the highlights. In the period 1914—1939 the *real* annual wages of the industrial workers rose by at least 50 %; the pay of the lumberman in northern Sweden almost tripled in thirty years, 1914—1944. The income of the farm workers has also risen but not at a comparable rate. The whitecollar workers in industry, commerce, and communications had received an average salary increase of 32 % by 1944, as compared to 1929, and the workmen in the same fields averaged a 55 % increase. If the real wage of an English industrial worker is set at 100, Sweden's corresponding figure would be 113, and the United States index considerably higher than that. An investigation similar to the one from which these figures were taken indicates that the daily wage of a farm worker is highest in England, the northern countries taking second place.

The Swede likes to telephone but not as much as the Dane or the Icelander. He often rides in an automobile and likes to dream about owning one. But while every fourth American has a car only every twenty-ninth Swede owns one. On the other hand, practically every grown Swede and older child has a bicycle. As a consumer of coffee, however, Sweden normally breaks all records and the coffee rationing was, understandably enough, one of the real wartime hardships. Tobacco is also an important item but the average Swede smokes less than half as much as the American. Alcoholic drinks, on the other hand, take a larger share of the private or family budget. But these and other social problems demand a separate chapter.

RÉSUMÉ OF
SWEDISH HISTORY

PREHISTORIC TIMES

THE VIKING AGE AND EARLY CHRISTIANITY

THE KALMAR UNION

THE AGE OF GUSTAV VASA

GUSTAF II ADOLF

SOCIAL CRISIS
— KARL XI's FINANCIAL REORGANIZATION

KARL XII

»ERA OF LIBERTY»
— INTRODUCTION OF PARLIAMENTARISM

THE GUSTAVIAN PERIOD

CONSTITUTIONAL DEVELOPMENT

EMIGRATION AND INDUSTRIALIZATION

UNIVERSAL SUFFRAGE

WORLD WAR II

61 and 62. Sweden is one of
the oldest countries in the world
still in existence. The unifica-
tion was begun by the Uppsala
kings (about 500 A. D.) whose
imposing burial mounds may be
seen at Gamla (Old) Uppsala.
Below: A stone with runic inscription from the Viking Age.
Photos by Gösta Lundquist.

69. Gustav III was one of the two great Swedish monarchs in the eighteenth century. His active support and patronage of art and literature were of great significance. This statue of the king, one of the noblest works in Swedish sculpture, was created by Johan Tobias Sergel. Photo by Lennart af Petersens.

PREHISTORIC TIMES

Eons ago all of Sweden was covered by an incredibly thick
ice cap. Fourteen thousand years have passed since it began
to melt away in the southern parts, and about twelve thousand
years ago the first primitive hunters began to follow the re-
ceding ice. Swedish geologists have made an intensive study
of the annual, stratified deposits of clay left by the ice and
have developed a dependable geochronic system. Thus we now
know that the southernmost parts of Sweden began to emerge
from the ice about 12 000 B.C. This is the oldest date in
Swedish history and perhaps the oldest dependable one in the
history of the world.

The primitive tribes who followed the ice as it withdrew
northward carried on the first and decisive struggle for a
settlement on Swedish soil. About 3 000 B. C. agriculture was
begun. Imposing tombs made with huge blocks of stone enable
us to trace the spread of this early peasant culture.

Copper and bronze became known about 1 500 B.C., and
the Bronze Age can be studied in the lavishly ornamented
weapons and adornments which have been preserved in the
soil. Common and extensive use of a metal in this early civilization was not possible until relations with countries to the south
had acquainted the northerners with iron, which they learned

to extract from bog ore found on the bottom of lakes and marshes. During the first centuries A.D. the provinces around Lake Mälaren and the *Suiones*, i. e. Svear, residing there began to assume their leading position. The first recorded mention of the *Suiones*, who were to give the whole country their name, is found in the *Germania* written by the Roman historian Tacitus in 98 A.D.

THE VIKING AGE AND EARLY CHRISTIANITY

The comparative isolation of Scandinavia was not broken until the Viking Age (700—1000 A.D.), when intrepid travelers brought back foreign goods and knowledge, new methods and new thoughts, in short, the contributions of more southerly civilizations. The coastal regions around and north of present-day Stockholm were the base of viking power and the starting point for great forays and trading expeditions—sometimes involving hundreds of ships—to the east. Whether as plunderers or merchants—and no clear distinction appears to have been made—the vikings kept up the contact between Sweden and the East (Russia, Constantinople), Sweden and Western Europe, including the British Isles and Ireland. The latter countries were the favorite goals of the men from southern Sweden who joined with Danish and Norwegian vikings, then their countrymen, in pillage, trade, or conquest.

Calmer centuries followed the viking expeditions and their tremendous display of energy. Eastern contacts ceased, and Sweden turned instead to the west and the south. Christianity gradually made headway with the aid of missions sent from England and northern Germany. Churches were built, first of wood, then of stone. Several hundreds of the latter from the twelfth and thirteenth centuries still stand. Sweden was incorporated in the huge organization of the Roman Catholic Church. At the same time the realm became more firmly established; it included Finland and all of modern Sweden, except the provinces of Blekinge, Bohuslän, Halland, and Skåne. Rival dynasties did not succeed in breaking the fundamental unity, definite procedures for electing the rulers were established, and a Council, drawn from the foremost families of the country, took its place by the king's side. Villages were expanded and new ones founded; in each century the frontier was pushed a little farther into the wilderness. During the thirteenth century the provincial statutes were compiled in law books which remain unique in their age and clarity. In these the life of the whole province was regulated in detail from the most elevated aspects to the commonest everyday concerns: "Christ is foremost in our law, next to Him our Christian dogma and all Christians: the King, farmers and all legal residents, bishops, all men of booklearning," but also "if horse rolls or swine roots in grainfield, (owner) pays fine therefor with such grain as was sown in the field, one skep for every third rolling or every third rooting." Differentiation into social groups took place in this period; in addition to the clergy a class of nobles emerged, the latter composed of estate owners and those high in the service of kings or lords. The nobles were exempt from taxes in exchange for military service in heavy armor.

On the island of Gotland the town of Visby developed into one of the strongest members in the Hanseatic League. Sweden thereby gained full entry to European trading and obtained an international market for her products, such as copper, iron, butter, and pelts. Soon after 1350 a national code was compiled. Based in part on the provincial laws, it aimed above all to safeguard peace and personal security. Acts of violence in church, at the thing-place (council meeting), in another man's house, or against a defenseless woman made a man an outlaw without rights and property. The "law of the land" included a brief constitution in which the powers of the king, the council, and the citizens were delimited. Even in the modern word order the duties of the king could hardly be defined more succinctly than in the old text: "The King shall all justice and truth strengthen, love and preserve, all wrongs and falsehoods destroy, both by law and by his royal power."

Strangely, the first Swede of international stature was a woman. Saint Birgitta (or Bridget; 1303—1373) is the greatest medieval figure in both the religious and the literary history of Sweden. She founded a monastic order which included both monks and nuns, and the first monastery was established at Vadstena. Visionary *(Revelationes)*, organizer (Order of St. Bridget), and unofficial envoy of Sweden in Rome for almost a quarter of a century, she had also found time to be a devoted wife and busy mistress of the family estates for twenty-seven years. A child-bride at thirteen, she bore her husband eight children, one of whom became Saint Catherine of Sweden.

THE KALMAR UNION

Late in the fourteenth century Queen Margareta, daughter of one king and widow of another, ruled both Denmark and Norway. A general reaction against growing German influence in the country, the Swedish king then being the German Albrekt of Mecklenburg, fear that their estates might be confiscated, and other circumstances prompted the Swedish nobles to appeal to Margareta for help against their own king. She defeated King Albrekt in battle in 1389 and became mistress of a united Scandinavia. Negotations conducted in the Swedish town of Kalmar in 1397 gave the union its name.

Margareta's kingdom was Europe's largest in area. As a noble experiment the unified realms showed foresight and statesmanship but after several decades of strife it failed nevertheless. Margareta's successor in 1412 (and nominal king since 1397), Erik of Pomerania, sought to extend the royal power throughout the triple realm and fought the German princes as well as the Hanseatic League while seeking political alliances in England and elsewhere. But Sweden was dependant on the Hanseatic League, especially in respect to a market for her metals; furthermore, the country was little inclined to tolerate increased tyrannical power on the part of the king.

In the mining districts of Bergslagen the people rose in revolt under the leadership of a simple mineowner by the name of Engelbrekt. The nobles, viewing with alarm the king's bid for greater power, made common cause with him. After bitter struggles between Denmark and Sweden the Union was dissolved. During these turbulent decades in the 15th century a notable innovation was made in the Swedish political system: the *Riksdag*, or Parliament, was instituted, which on behalf of the people made important political decisions. Even the farmers were represented in this new body.

Kristian II, king of Denmark since 1513, soon became a new threat to Sweden's independence. Hope of a successful defense against the repeated attacks faded when the Swedish regent, Sten Sture the Younger, fell in one of the losing battles against the Danes in 1520. By the "Stockholm Massacre," a mass execution in the conquered capital, Kristian attempted to eliminate the leaders of the independence party and with them all opposition. Once more it appeared that a great northern kingdom was in formation, this time by violence. But the king had underestimated the Swedish tradition of freedom.

THE AGE OF GUSTAV VASA

A revolt against the Danish king, led by a yong, rather unknown relative of the Stures, Gustav Eriksson Vasa, began in Dalarna in 1520—1521. He definitely put an end to the Union and made Sweden into a national state of the type which had arisen on the Continent during the late Middle Ages. His features are familiar to every Swede and also become known to foreign visitors, for his portrait appears on all Swedish paper money.

Gustav Vasa placed the stamp of his personality on Sweden's history from 1523, when at the age of twenty-seven he was elected to the throne, and until his death in 1560. His first royal concern was the stabilization of the state finances; by resolute measures at the Västerås *Riksdag* in 1527 he created the conditions necessary for the confiscation by the state of all property in the hands of the Roman Catholic Church. Since at the end of the Middle Ages the Church held 21 % of the Swedish soil, as compared with only 5.6 % owned by the Crown, this represented an immense addition to the strength of the state. Gustav Vasa found a certain amount of justification for this measure in the Lutheran teachings which had begun to spread in the country with the full approval of the king. Gradually the Swedish Church was separated from Rome, became Lutheran in character, and was organized into a State Church which survives to this day. The decree of the Västerås Parliament established the new religious phase with the goodly statement that "the plain and true word of God shall be preached in the realm." Simultaneously with the great confiscation of church property the king and his men reorganized the government administration and developed unprecedented efficiency. Various provinces, such as Dalarna and Småland, objected strenuously to having their local interests set aside for the common good. When they rebelled against the king, they were severely castigated. Foundations for modern literature were also laid during the reign of Gustav Vasa with a complete translation of the Bible and in the hymns and theological writings of Olaus Petri, Swedish reformer.

For half a century his sons, Erik XIV, Johan III, and Karl IX, ruled Sweden in the order named. All three were interesting, talented, but contradictory men, engrossed in the confusing international relations of the day. From the south Denmark plotted against Sweden, while the Swedes repeatedly waged successive wars against Lübeck, Poland, and Russia. One of their more consistent efforts was to gain control over Russia's foreign trade in the Baltic Sea, to which she had no direct access. When Estonia became Swedish in 1595 this objective was partly attained, for Sweden thereby obtained considerable strength in the Baltic area and control over some of the important trade routes to Russia.

A new attempt at a north-European union was made by Sigismund, son of Johan III, who through his mother first became king of Poland, then in 1592 succeeded his father on the throne of Sweden. His Catholicism and prolonged absences in Poland caused great opposition in Sweden and paved the way for his uncle Karl to depose him in 1599. The only consequence of Sigismund's abortive enterprise was that acute enmity replaced the former alliance between the two countries. Karl remained protector of the realm and did not assume the title of King Karl IX until 1604. During the last years before his death in 1611 Sweden was waging a losing struggle against Denmark, Poland, and Russia. The situation looked dark indeed.

GUSTAV II ADOLF

Sweden's greatest expansion grew out of the ensuing struggle for existence. Even Karl IX's campaigns against Sigismund and Poland had acquired an expansionist character, but the new conflict spread to include all of Europe in the Thirty Years' War. The House of Habsburg was in the process of crushing the Protestant princes in Germany and advanced toward the Baltic with the intent of becoming a great power also in northern Europe. Gustaf Adolf decided to participate in the historic struggle. He first launched an attack against the heart of Poland and seized the most important towns in eastern Prussia, which were vital to Poland's commerce. Then he led his army into Germany against Habsburg and the Catholic League, received support from France, and in 1631 routed the famous General Tilly in the battle of Breitenfeld (near Leipzig) in Saxony. The next winter he held court in Mainz and Frankfurt a. M., marched through Bavaria in the summer of 1632, and on the 6th of November that year encountered Wallenstein, the Emperor's chief commander, at Lützen, not far from Breitenfeld. Wallenstein was forced to retreat, but Gustav Adolf fell in the battle.

An almost inevitable question presents itself as these extensive campaigns are reviewed: How could a small country like Sweden, modest in its resources, generate and maintain such military power?

Throughout the war the king had the people's approval.

Parliament, including nobles, clergy, burghers, and peasants, had been in full accord with him on the necessity of entering the war in Germany. In presenting and justifying his plans and actions before the representatives of the people the king was indefatigable. His armies were largely composed of Swedish farmers, their sons and hands. A source of financial support was the copper mine at Falun, whose exports were then in great demand throughout Europe. The political genius of Gustav II Adolf, his talent for military organization, and his advanced ideas on strategy and tactics were important, contributory factors in the success of his campaigns. In addition, the king possessed outstanding administrative ability.

When Gustav Adolf fell, his heir and only daughter Kristina was six years old. The regency was placed in the hands of a group from the upper nobility, headed by Chancellor Axel Oxenstierna, Sweden's greatest statesman. For sixteen more years the war in Germany continued. The Peace of Westphalia (1648) gave to Sweden a number of important possessions on the southern shore of the Baltic and on the North Sea, but the Polish ports had to be relinquished; in addition, the Catholic German states were to pay reparations.

Sweden's strategic position was wholly changed.—Queen Kristina was succeeded by her cousin, Karl X Gustav, who was waging war in Poland, when Denmark joined Sweden's enemies. He then departed from Poland with his army in 1658, marched through Schleswig-Holstein and forced the Danes to transfer to Sweden the provinces of Blekinge, Skåne, Halland, and Bohuslän. In a surprise move the king had led his army over the newly frozen Belts—one of history's most daring exploits—and Denmark had to relinquish her control over The Sound, main inlet to the Baltic Sea.

SOCIAL CRISIS—KARL XI's FINANCIAL REORGANIZATION

Since that time the southern provinces have remained Swedish and represent the lasting gain from the period of power politics. However, this policy also had a very negative aspect. A large portion of the monies and much of the support needed for the wars had been secured through the transfer or sale of crown lands or tax concessions to the nobility. In a country still having an economy largely operating in kind, it was necessary to resort to such means. European power politics could not, after all, be financed with taxes paid in butter and grain. The result was that the nobles ended up with the possession of about 72 % of Sweden's soil, while the Crown and the independent farmers had to be satisfied with the remaining 28 %. Those farmers who had become subject to the nobles and paid their taxes to them obviously had difficulty in maintaining any measure of independence, especially since the lords in question had acquired on the Continent a purely feudal attitude toward subordinates. Enormous as the growth was in respect to wealth and political influence on the part of the nobles, it had its justification in the brilliant contributions made by them during the war period. Nevertheless, it became a source of danger to the existence of free husbandmen as well as to the central government authorities.

Sweden's Vasa kings had not always seen eye to eye with the nobles. Gustav Vasa's three sons had severe clashes and sanguinary reckonings with them. Gustav II Adolf had maintained good cooperation with the great men of the realm, but for his daughter, Kristina, the situation was more difficult. To curb the nobles, restore order in the state finances after the wars, and assist the farmers in the struggle for their ancient freedoms combined into an immense task even for as talented a woman ruler as Kristina. Furthermore, her personal position was changed when she secretly became a convert to Catholicism. She found herself in a complex quandary of conscience and decided to abdicate, but not until she had secured the throne for her cousin, Karl Gustav, and forestalled his being faced with increased power on the part of the nobility. The almost constant wars and his early death (1660) at the age of thirty-eight prevented Karl X Gustav too from solving the great internal problems. During the long regency for his minor son, Karl XI, the influence of the nobles grew even more. Early in Karl XI's own reign, which began in 1672, he had to lead a bitter struggle against Denmark for the retention of the southern provinces. When peace was concluded in 1679, the king began a gigantic task of reorganization reminiscent of Gustav Vasa's a century and a half earlier. This is customarily referred to as Karl XI's "reduction," i. e. by vote of Parliament the nobles were "reduced" as the Crown repossessed a large part of the estates they had obtained for themselves. At the end of this reorganization the property distribution was once more radically changed, the Crown now held 35.6 % of the soil, the nobles only 32.9 % and the independent farmers 31.5 %. In accordance with a detailed plan, the king used the income from state properties to cover all expenses of the Crown, such as the military and civil service payrolls. An important by-product of the reorganization was that the status of the free farmers was restored and secured. However, the nobles retained their extensive privileges, but their rule was replaced by that of an absolute monarch.

A few years of peace quickened the economic life of the nation. Copper had declined in importance, but iron exports had increased, and wood tar also became a major item in the shipments abroad at the time. This peaceful period gave Karl XI an opportunity to carry out his sometimes harsh but generally beneficial reforms. They affected every phase of Swedish life: commerce, finances, defenses, legal procedures, the state church, education.

KARL XII

Nearly two decades of peace under Karl XI were followed by the last major war period in Sweden's history. Upon the death of his father in 1697, Karl XII, just past fifteen, at the urging of Parliament ascended the throne as ruling and absolute monarch.

Two years later the storm broke as Sweden was threatened by a triple attack; Russia, Poland-Saxony, and Denmark declared war, and Sweden's situation seemed as difficult as it had been a hundred years earlier. In brilliant victories—the most famous in 1700 at Narva against Russian forces ten times as great—Karl crossed the plans of the hostile coalition, eliminated Denmark, gave the Czar the setback at Narva, pursued the Polish King August through Poland, and forced the Peace of Altranstädt in 1706.

A bold expedition against Russia's heart in 1709 anticipated the trail of both Napoleon and Hitler; in each case the outcome was about the same. It led to Karl's defeat at Poltava, the capitulation of his army, and his own flight to Turkey. There he was virtually interned for years, during which he was partly successful in persuading the Turks to attack Russia. The home country held out against the extended coalition which now included Russia, Saxony, Denmark, Hanover, England, and Prussia. In 1715 the king managed to return to Sweden.

Karl pinned his hopes on the Anglo-Russian rivalry, but in the midst of complicated diplomatic maneuvers he was killed as he besieged the Norwegian fortress of Fredriksten (near Fredrikshald) in 1718. Sweden then had to conclude a series of peace treaties which left her with few of her far-flung possessions, except most of Finland and a couple of small holdings on the south shore of the Baltic.

"ERA OF LIBERTY"—INTRODUCTION OF PARLIAMENTARISM

A total but almost bloodless revolution to establish a new constitution was the first internal move after the collapse. This document gave by far the greatest authority to Parliament, whose wishes were carried out by the king and his council. In the council the king had only two votes, and he was himself elected to the throne by Parliament.

The "Era of Liberty," as the next fifty-three years are called, has been severely criticized for its partisan animosity and political befuddlement. But it has become increasingly clear that this era was of great significance in shaping the Swedish heritage of freedom. A real parliamentary system was gradually developed, which to be sure labored under very heavy and cumbersome, juridically formulated procedures. Nevertheless, it is of great interest in many respects and a notable parallel to the English system.

Two parties, the "Hats" and the "Caps," came into being and contended for the political power. In their theories of national economy the Hats were strictly mercantilistic. Their foreign policy aimed at an alliance with France whereby they hoped to regain the foreign possessions recently lost; this led to badly prepared wars and correspondingly unfortunate outcomes.

The Caps were more restrained in respect to state subsidies in the national economy and their foreign policy strove for rapprochement with England and Russia. Toward the end of the era the Caps also gathered into their ranks the commoners in opposition to the prerogatives of the nobles.

Alternately in power—the Hats being at the helm somewhat longer—the two parties developed far-reaching assumptions regarding the authority of Parliament. "The idea that the Estates (of Parliament) may err is contrary to the fundamental law of the realm" is a sample of their claims; if the king refused to sign the council decisions, it was not unheard of that a facsimile stamp of the royal signature was used. During these years af acrid party feuds, however, a truly significant political development took place which proved of great importance to the subsequent evolution of the Swedish constitution. Considerable economic and cultural progress also distinguishes the era. Land reforms came under discussion, there was an interest in the advancement of the frontiers of science, and the Swedish press was born. Carl von Linné (Linnaeus) created his botanical classification system, and Emanuel Swedenborg his unique philosophy of religion.

THE GUSTAVIAN PERIOD

Violent struggles over the prerogatives of the nobility flared up during the last years of the Era of Liberty. The foreign policy of the Hats had cost Sweden a part of Finland. A certain weariness with the constant tug-of-war between the two parties was in evidence. All in all, a number of circumstances paved the way for a new *coup d'état*.

Gustav III, a nephew of Prussia's Frederick the Great,

ascended the throne in 1771. The following year he placed himself at the head of the forces opposed to the *status quo,* and the ensuing revolution took place without bloodshed. A new constitution accorded the king greater power, but parliamentary opposition, especially on the part of the politically powerful nobility, was not to be downed. Consequently, in the midst of a provoked and ill-conducted war with Russia, Gustav III put over a second *coup* which increased the royal prerogatives to such an extent that the next twenty years (1789—1809) are referred to as the "Gustavian Absolutism." Gustav III himself was assassinated three years later (1792) by a fanatic group of young noblemen in the opposition. A patron of literature and the arts, endowed with brilliant personal qualities, Gustav III remains one of the most captivating and colorful figures in the whole succession of Swedish rulers.

This period brought certain important reforms, among them an equalization of civil rights and a fundamental land act, but the external events became predominant. In 1805 Gustav IV Adolf, son and heir of Gustav III, had chosen to side with England in the contest for supremacy among the great powers. Thus Sweden was drawn into the struggle against Napoleon and soon found herself in an extremely precarious situation. The king took this step with an eye to England's great importance in Sweden's foreign trade and stood firm in spite of Napoleon's overwhelming success. The outcome was something resembling a catastrophe.

In the treaty of Tilsit (1807), Napoleon gave his new ally, Alexander I of Russia, free hand to proceed against Sweden, hoping to force her into the camp of England's enemies. The aim was to make the Continental Blockade against England wholly effective. As Gustav IV Adolf remained loyal to his ally, Russia fell upon Finland, which was lost in its entirety (1809). Gustav IV Adolf's ability was by no means great enough to meet the crisis, and his temperament further emphasized the absolute nature of his office. In the eyes of the public officials, the military, and all liberty-professing citizens he became the scapegoat for the unhappy outcome and was removed in a new revolution, also in 1809, again without bloodshed. A new constitution was adopted, which in its fundamental features is still in effect, and the deposed king's uncle became ruler as Karl XIII.

CONSTITUTIONAL DEVELOPMENT

Since 1521 Sweden had undergone six major dynastic or constitutional readjustments, the last four without bloodshed. Within the same three hundred years she went through three sweeping changes of a social nature, for the most part peacefully. Gustav Vasa's confiscation of church property and Karl XI's repossession of crown lands have already been traced; the third social change spanned the years 1719—1809 and may be described as a gradual and more equitable redistribution of rights and privileges.

What the French Revolution achieved by means of numerous violent upheavals came about undramatically but quite effectively in Sweden. For example, the farmers obtained the right to purchase clear title to crown lands. Commoners could own exempt land and were admitted even to high government posts previously held only by nobles. Several of these innovations were made by Gustav III. Some archaic elements remained in the constitution and the societal structure, however, and the political struggles of the nineteenth century pivoted to a large extent around them.

In the Constitution of 1809 the attempt was made to profit

from previous experience in achieving a balance among the various authorities, king, cabinet, parliament, and government officials. The success of this attempt depended in part on the leaders involved.

Karl XIII was childless, and a successor had to be found outside the dynasty. The final choice was one of Napoleon's famous marshals, Bernadotte, who became Crown Prince Karl Johan when he set foot on Swedish soil in 1810. By having his adopted country participate in the last coalition against Napoleon, he obtained compensation of a sort for the loss of Finland. In exchange for Swedish Pomerania, the last of Sweden's possessions in northern Germany, Denmark was forced to relinquish Norway to Sweden. The Norwegians protested, chose their own king, and drew up a new constitution for themselves. They were finally compelled to accept a union with Sweden in 1814, but their virtual independence and the recently adopted constitution were both recognized. This chain of events gained considerable authority for Karl Johan, and his personal influence buttressed the royal power. On the death of the old king in 1818, the French marshal and former sergeant became Karl XIV Johan.

There was growing class consciousness on the part of the "middle class" which had emerged during the past hundred years. It included modern entrepreneurs in commerce, agriculture, and such industry as existed. Within the framework of the constitution a struggle now ensued concerning public influence on the country's administration, and liberal opinion really came to the fore in the 1840's. In the reigns of Oscar I and Karl XV—son and grandson, respectively, of Karl XIV Johan—a series of reforms were carried out. Most important among these was the change in national representation of 1865. It abolished the four Estates—nobles, clergy, burghers, and peasants—of which the Swedish Parliament had traditionally been composed as no longer representative of the existing social structure. Instead the *Riksdag* was to have two elected chambers. Free enterprise became a normal part of the Swedish system in 1846, free trade in the 1860's. Public schools and free education became general in 1842, and the manufacture of alcoholic liquors was restricted in 1854.

EMIGRATION AND INDUSTRIALIZATION

The greatest changes in nineteenth century Sweden are of such a nature that they cannot be traced in terms of specific dates. Since the middle of the eighteenth century the population had increased rapidly—it had approximately doubled by 1850—and the country's resources could not keep the pace. To be sure, it had been possible to modernize agriculture by means of the already mentioned land reforms of the early nineteenth century. The ancient village units, whose collective work methods did not meet modern demands, were divided by the Enclosure Act into "individually operating farms." Much new land was broken or reclaimed and work procedures were rationalized. But these gains in land and efficiency still could not keep up with a constantly growing population. A rural proletariat came into being, whose serious problems hardly permitted any solution.

This became the background for a great emigration, which began in the middle of the nineteenth century and culminated in the 1880's. The goal for most of those who left was the United States, where more space and greater opportunities beckoned. In the 1880's, a decade of agricultural depression, an alarming total of 347 000 Swedes emigrated; 46 900 departed in the peak year (1887). In America the emigrants

142

frequently settled all-Swedish communities, some of which still exist as such. They often sought out territory which in climate, terrain, and resources resembled the home province and thus offered similar opportunities for earning a livelihood; the preponderantly Swedish communities in north central United States are in many ways reminiscent of Sweden. The greatest concentration of Swedish emigrants settled in the area west of Lake Michigan as far out as the Rocky Mountains, from the southern edge of Kansas up to the Canadian border. Naturally, Swedes in smaller numbers are found in all parts of the United States.

Their early predecessors were the already mentioned Swedes who in 1638 established a Swedish colony, New Sweden, near the present city of Wilmington on the Delaware. A descendant of these first Swedish-Americans was John Morton, co-signatory to the Declaration of Independence.

Gradually the tide of emigration receded, largely as a result of another major change in the societal structure. The beginnings of modern industry had been in evidence as early as the middle of the nineteenth century. In the lead were the forest industries; demand for lumber from the great Swedish stands was soon found abroad, as modern, steam-powered sawmills were erected. Industrialization proceeded at a more rapid rate from about 1870 and definitely reached the front rank in the national economy around 1890. As indicated in the geographical summary, parts of ancient, agricultural Sweden became modern industrial regions. Formerly the frontier could be moved only by breaking new land or working new mines. Now, however, man could penetrate into the remotest wilderness and exploit its long-hidden resources. Added to this were the metal industries previously described and other manufacturing activity. New technological processes were at last developed which toward the end of the nineteenth century made the formerly worthless, high-phosphorus ore of northern Sweden with its high iron content an important export staple.

Parallel with this economic revolution—the greatest in Sweden's history since the establishment of agriculture in the Stone Age—a new and extensive social change was taking place; the term "popular movements" is commonly used to describe it. The great groups of the population who did not have the suffrage—and only 9.5 % were entitled to vote even in the beginning of the twentieth century!—began to seek other outlets for their energy and new ways to exert an influence on the society in which they lived. They found such outlets in the religious revival movements in the middle of the century; in the labor movement, which grew rapidly during the decades of industrialization and early embraced social democracy as its political faith; in the temperance movements, which became a great force in the social training and education of the so-called lower classes; and later they turned to the cooperative movement and organized sports. In a later chapter on modern life in Sweden, we shall consider in more detail the nature of these movements and of the organizations gradually created by them.

UNIVERSAL SUFFRAGE

The social trend just mentioned and the general concern of the people with problems of national interest led to a whole series of constitutional changes and social reforms. When the union with Norway was dissolved in 1905—another major adjustment made in a peaceable and dignified manner—solution of the internal problems became even more urgent. A

144

franchise reform in 1907 doubled the electorate from 9.5 % to 19 % of the total population. Complete democracy with universal suffrage for men and women, making over 54 % of the citizens voters, was achieved in 1918. Political parties in the modern sense began to emerge late in the last century; they were strong and active in the early decades of the present one. Parliamentarism first came to the fore in modern times in 1905 and became definitively established in 1917. Social welfare legislation began in earnest early in the present century and started to make rapid strides along partly new lines of approach in the 1930's. Its progress will be described in more detail later. The results were achieved on the basis of a general debate in which all of the parties of the *Riksdag*—Conservatives, Liberals, and Social Democrats—participated.

Most heatedly discussed were the problems of labor and unemployment. The creation of a modern military establishment was begun toward the end of the nineteenth century but later became the subject of very conflicting opinions. Real unity of purpose was not attained until the 1930's and then under the pressure of the dictatorship to the south.

The great social and economic changes taking place since the middle of the last century were achieved along constitutional and legislative line without violent upheavals. Sometimes they were slow and deliberate but by way of compensation well considered and in harmony with the legal heritage of Sweden.

WORLD WAR II

During the second world war Sweden was placed in a difficult and delicate position. Looking back for a moment over the pre-war period, an observer would note that Sweden and her people had been interested and loyal participants in the League of Nations during the 20's. They felt that the country should earn and maintain her place as an active member of the organization which held the promise of peace and international cooperation. Gradually, however, Sweden moved back to a line of strict neutrality, a position she had taken during the first world war. True, in the few years immediately before the new outbreak of war certain steps had been taken toward a northern or north-European bloc ("Oslo States," 1937) but they were minor in consequence. Work on the country's defenses had been under way since 1936 and was further speeded when the threat of a catastrophe became increasingly clear.

When the war actually commenced, Sweden in concurrence with the other northern countries issued a declaration of neutrality which almost immediately had to meet its first test during the Finno-Russian war in the winter 1939—1940. A strong political popular movement in favor of Finland's cause then made itself felt but did not result in any official participation in the conflict. On the other hand, a number of volunteers joined the Finnish forces, and Sweden placed extensive material aid at Finland's disposal. When later the Allies, primarily England, wished to send troops through Sweden to aid Finland (March 1940), the request was refused. This was motivated by the government's desire to avoid having the country drawn into the conflict between the great powers. Toward the end of the "winter war" Sweden undertook the role of mediator between the two belligerents.

Close on the heels of the Finno-Russian armistice came the German occupation of Denmark and the attack on Norway (April 9, 1940). German plans to attack Sweden as well were known to exist; Sweden's rearmament was not completed and her strategic situation extremely difficult. That Sweden at that time did not share her neighbors' fate of being attacked by

Germany can hardly be fully explained even now. It is known, however, that Russia advised the German high command against an invasion of Sweden. It became a serious problem to resist the German demands for permission to send military transports over Swedish territory against the defenders of Norway. Such demands were repeatedly turned down in April and May, 1940, and only Red Cross transports to northern Norway were permitted. "Since the hostilities in Norway had ceased" the government later felt restrained to permit transit of military equipment and personnel on leave between Norway and Germany via Sweden. This decision was probably dictated by the extremely difficult strategic position in which Sweden now more than ever found herself. Furthermore, the Swedish defense preparations were not yet completed. The government and the high command consequently at that time felt that a hopeless war with Germany was unavoidable, if the demands were refused. In many quarters the reaction of public opinion was very strong. A popular movement in behalf of Norway's cause gathered numerous supporters in the months that followed, and it may be stated that the Swedish people were deeply aware of a strain on their conscience in this tragic situation.

The government was forced to make one more major concession to the nazis. Just before the German attack on Russia in June, 1941, the transfer of a German division from Norway to Finland over Swedish territory was permitted. Further requests of that nature were refused.

During these grave years public opinion in Sweden was almost wholly on the Allied side. What became known about German oppression in Norway strengthened this attitude besides causing resentment and sorrow.

The Swedish people had to realize that they were living on an almost entirely isolated and threatened, but still independent isle in the north-European sphere of German conquest. Only with great difficulty was it possible to tide the nation over the shortages, as extensive rationing was put into effect and a speedy conversion of the industries undertaken. Ships given safe conduct by both belligerent sides maintained some contact with the outside world, and a certain amount of trade was carried on with Germany. The latter involved mostly the export of iron ore, the import of coal and chemicals, an exchange necessary for Swedish rearmament, the easing of shortages, and the production of many important consumer goods. On April 9, 1940, about one half of the Swedish merchant marine was in foreign waters outside the German blockade; this tonnage was chartered to England and the United States.

An intensive debate on the foreign policy was conducted during this period by both the Swedish press and the citizenry. Frequently the question was whether the concessions made to the peremptory requests of the Germans had been necessary and whether still more refusals could have been risked, for many of their demands had been firmly declined time and again. These discussions repeatedly led to violent tantrums on the part of Hitler and his henchmen; in order to avoid charges of provocation, parliament in 1941 decided on a limited press censorship, imposed when "at war or in danger of war." Although it never was imposed, it created the constitutional means of applying censorship in case of need. In any event the nazi press continued to pour a steady stream of coarse invectives upon Sweden and her newspapers—most outspoken was the Göteborg *Commerce and Shipping News (Göteborgs Handels-och Sjöfartstidning)* edited by Torgny Segerstedt—because of their anti-German stand and the public opinion they reflected.

During the final stages of the European war Sweden became increasingly active in humanitarian work. Much had, of course, been done ever since the outbreak of hostilities; thus in

1939—1940 during the "winter war" many Finnish children were received and cared for in Swedish homes. When the Germans attacked Norway, a stream of refugees began to flow into Sweden and finally totalled about 50 000. Some of these went on to Allied countries; around 5 800 went by air to England. At the end of the occupation in Denmark the Danish refugees numbered about 18 000. Some of the Norwegians and Danes were also trained in Sweden for later military police duty, fully equipped, and armed. Guns and ammunition were cached along the boundaries or sent into the neighboring countries to aid the resistance movements. The refugees in Sweden were given collective permits to obtain work and became a welcome addition to the short labor supply.

Large numbers of refugees from the Baltic countries to the east were also admitted during the war years. When the nazi pogroms against Danish Jews began, approximately 7 500 found asylum in Sweden. King Gustav addressed an effective personal plea to the nazi "government" in Budapest, asking for humane treatment of the Hungarian Jews. The Swedish Legation in Budapest attracted international attention as emergency passports were issued to thousands of persecuted Jews. Main spring in this action of mercy was Raoul Wallenberg, who disappeared (January, 1945) and presumably had to give his life for this cause. After long and intricate negotiations with the Germans it became possible to extend further aid in an unexpected manner. Count Folke Bernadotte (1895—1948), a nephew of the king, was able in the spring of 1945 to remove the Danes and Norwegians—and later prisoners of other nationalities—from the German concentration camps and transport them to Sweden. He acted for the Swedish Red Cross, and a caravan of its busses carried out the adventurous plan. In such ways many victims of nazism were rescued, given care, and started on the road to rehabilitation.

Sweden's neutrality thus in some respects worked to the advantage of Denmark, Norway, and several other countries. A report from the Swedish prime minister, Per Albin Hansson (d. 1946), stated there was good reason to suppose that the ever more earnest representations from the Swedish government had prevented additional outrages on the part of the Germans in both Denmark and Norway. On the whole, however, the Swedish foreign policy during the war years was the subject of much adverse criticism. The Swedish government felt called upon to issue a "White Book" with detailed explanations and facts pertaining to the course taken.

GOVERNMENT AND
POLITICAL LIFE

THE GOVERNMENT AND ITS TRADITIONS

THE LEGAL SYSTEM

POLITICAL PARTIES

THE PRESS

THE GOVERNMENT AND ITS
TRADITIONS

In the preceding account of Sweden's history and economic life it has been shown that Swedish democracy is well rooted in traditions several centuries old. Ever since the first recording of the provincial laws about seven hundred years ago an uninterrupted constitutional tradition has existed. Parliament, in which the peasants also had their representatives from the very beginning, dates back to the fifteenth century. Still older is the institution of the king's council, which time and again has held its own against autocratically inclined rulers. Sweden's oldest written constitution, brief though it be, is about six hundred years old. It is included in the provincial law under the section dealing with the kingship and establishes the principles of peace and justice as valid for government authorities and individual citizen alike. Sometimes absolute monarchy, sometimes a powerful and egoistic high nobility has threatened the people's liberty. But, on the other hand, Karl XI's absolutism contributed toward the preservation of the freedom of the farmers, and the high nobility defended the free constitution against the king both during the time of the Kalmar Union and on later occasions. Each threat was voided, and time and again freedom was recaptured and reestablished.

The Constitution

Sweden's earliest experience with parliamentarism occured during a fifty-year period in the eighteenth century. It came to nought, and the modern version was not fully developed until the present century was under way. However, the Constitution of 1809—with all the amendments made from time to time—is still in force and now the oldest in Europe. To the basic Constitution Act *(Regeringsformen)* of 1809, which defines the essential organization, duties, and powers of the national government, three fundamental acts have since been added. When Marshal Bernadotte was elected Swedish crown prince, the Succession Act (*Successionsordningen*, 1810) was passed to establish the sequence of future rulers. The Freedom of the Press Act (*Tryckfrihetsförordningen*, 1812) guarantees the right implied in its title and also grants public access to certain government records and documents. A new and improved version of the Freedom of the Press Act was tentatively accepted by the *Riksdag* in 1948. The Parliament Act *(Riksdagsordningen*, 1866) abolished the ancient four estates in favor of a bicameral body and defined the procedures and powers of the new organization.

The Swedish constitution is a legal and technical rather than a popular document. An amendment must be passed by two independently elected parliaments, i. e. in two sessions with a general election intervening; some of the minor constitutional provisions are revised or added in almost every annual session.

The Monarchy

With the exception of about fifty years of rule by regents around 1500, Sweden has always had a king in historical times. The voice of a free people through their representatives has normally found the monarch with a willing ear; if not, that voice has often asserted itself. The earliest reference to a popular, deliberative assembly in Sweden is found in the *Travels* of Ansgar, the "Apostle of the North," in the ninth century. He also tells of the king who ruled at Birka, trading center and capital, where Ansgar freely preached the Word of God.

Gustav V, the present king, has a strong claim to recognition and admiration at home and abroad on many scores. His reign, which completed the fourth decade in December, 1947, is the longest in Sweden's history. As a man and as a king he holds the highest regard in the public consciousness. In his long life he has experienced the complete democratization of the constitution and the evolution of the modern parliamentary system in Sweden.

The Cabinet

The Cabinet, or State Council, is also of ancient lineage; in its oldest form it appeared as early as the thirteenth century. By the Constitution of 1634 the Cabinet was reorganized and remained largely unchanged until 1809. As already indicated, this body played a very important part in the destiny of the nation during the party rule of the Era of Liberty.

Sweden's present Cabinet is composed of a Prime Minister, eleven Department Ministers, and four Ministers without portfolio. Cabinet ministers need not be members of the *Riksdag* but in all matters have the right to address either Chamber. One or more times a week they meet in preliminary cabinet session *(statsrådsberedningen)*, a practice not mentioned in the Constitution. In these, however, the attitude of the Government on all major questions is determined. The ministers are equal in rank, and all of them participate in these preliminary meetings. The formal decisions are made in the weekly cabinet session at the Royal Palace, at which the King presides *(konselj)*. The powers of the Crown are vested in the King-in-Council. Each minister proposes his departmental items for the agenda and countersigns the King's signature on decisions and legislation pertinent to his department. Only in rare and exceptional cases is the King likely to oppose the wishes of the Cabinet. This collective responsibility of the cabinet ministers is a distinctive feature of the Swedish governmental system. Ministerial government, in the sense that the department heads have the right to make independent decisions, has no legal basis, except in regard to certain routine matters. However, the functions of the government have multiplied to such an extent that the department heads have of necessity been invested with considerable powers to act independently.

On a sculptured frieze (picture nr 71) in the government building where the cabinet offices are located, *Kanslihuset*, Stig Blomberg, leading Swedish sculptor, has depicted some of the areas of departmental activity, including foreign affairs, justice, defense, social affairs, communications, finance, public worship and education, agriculture, commerce, and national economy. Incidentally, a Department of the Interior has now been instituted to handle certain areas formerly under the Department of Social Affairs.

A cabinet change occurs when the parliament majority does not share the cabinet attitude on important issues, or when a general election has indicated a shift in public opinion. Under this parliamentary system, the King asks one political party, normally the one with the majority in Parliament, to form the new government. Up to 1932 a system of minority government was in effect, since several parties, none of which occupied an absolutely dominant position, opposed each other

70. Gustav V, king of Sweden, in the procession on his ninetieth birthday, June 16, 1948.
Seated in the lap of Princess Sibylla is the two-year-old Hereditary Prince Carl-Gustav.
Photo by Text & Bilder.

71. Blomberg's relief in the Government Office Building, symbolizing the historical development of the various departments. Reading from left, top frieze symbolizes the Departments of Justice, Social Welfare, and Public Worship and Education. Center frieze: The Departments of Finance and Agriculture. Bottom frieze: The Departments of Commerce and Communications.

72 and 73. Every Friday the King meets with the cabinet officers. Decisions reached here are signed by the king in person. The adjoining picture shows an interior from the Lower House. Photos by Bertil Norberg and Lennart af Petersens.

in Parliament. Possibilities of a minority government still exist, for five political parties are active in Sweden.

From time to time Sweden has had coalition governments composed of Social Democrats and Farmer Unionists or Liberals. In time of crisis a "national" government may be organized with representatives from all parties. This was done in 1905 when the union with Norway was dissolved and again during World War II.

Parliament

The Swedish Parliament has a somewhat later origin than the Cabinet but is still one of the oldest in the world. As already mentioned, it came into being as such in the fifteenth century—1435 is the date frequently mentioned—but has older traditions, among them the provincial assemblies which elected the kings a hundred years earlier.

In its modern form, Parliament consists of two Houses or Chambers, both elected. The entire Lower House stands for election every fourth year by direct vote of men and women over twenty-one. The term of tenure in the Upper House is eight years; one eighth of the members stand for election every year by indirect vote, the electors being the county and town councils, who, in turn, are chosen in general communal elections. Proportional representation is used throughout. A candidate for the Upper House must be at least thirty-five years old, for the Lower House at least twenty-five. There are 150 members in the former chamber, 230 in the latter.

In respect to occupation and social class the members of Parliament constitute a rather faithful cross-section of the general population. Professional politicians are few and play a comparatively minor role, but their number seems to be on the increase. One cause for this trend may be the fact that in

161

recent years Parliament has been in session the greater part of the year while formerly it convened for a spring session only.

The majority of items on the parliament agenda are submitted by the Cabinet in the form of government or "royal" proposals *(proposition)*. Groups or individual members of Parliament also submit their own bills *(motion)*.

Perhaps the procedure can best be illustrated by tracing an example. A member has had his attention drawn, say, to a social problem which he feels should be solved by legislation. On his own, or with some colleagues, he presents his bill, which then is referred by both Houses to a committee. The committee system, by the way, is very characteristic of the Swedish Parliament and dates back to the seventeenth century. Since most of the work is done in committee rather than in debates from the floor, a number of standing committees are maintained and special ones may be appointed to handle major problems. Members are drawn from both chambers and are, as a rule, reelected, thus gradually giving each committee a large fund of knowledge and experience in its particular area.

The proper committee studies our hypothetical proposal, gathers information, including the comments of experts, from various quarters, and then submits an opinion to Parliament. Should the committee find itself unable to complete a survey of the problem or faced with too complicated an issue, it may propose that the Cabinet be requested to have an investigation made. Such an investigation may also be proposed by any member of Parliament. If this is done, the government appoints a Royal Commission of one or more experts plus representatives of the major parties. After due investigation this body submits a report which then is transmitted to government bureaus, authorities, and organizations which might be affected by the proposal. On the basis of all the material gathered, the government decides whether the issue in question shall be presented to Parliament. If the bill is submitted to Parliament in the form of a government proposal, the committee once more reviews the matter before Parliament makes a decision. In case the proposal passes, the Cabinet draws up the necessary statute, which then is signed by the King and countersigned by the Minister in whose department the issue was classified.

Urgent issues occur, of course, which leave no time for so deliberate a process. The procedure may be shortened but, in any case, every issue receives careful attention, and both Houses must be agreed for a decision to be reached. Financial issues rejected by the one chamber or the other may be reconsidered with minimum delay by means of a joint revote. Parliament can increase or decrease appropriations proposed by the government as well as advocate new ones for other purposes.

Thoroughness is obviously a characteristic of this parliamentary system, based as it is on the direct cooperation of all political parties. Cavilers may call it dilatory, but to the average citizen it is indicative of stable procedure and fair-minded legislation.

Central Administrative Boards

In most countries the central administration is organized as a system of instruments or agencies at the disposal of the ministers and under their immediate direction. This does not, however, accurately describe Swedish institutions. Legally speaking, since the seventeenth century, Sweden has had two distinct elements in the central administration: the king with his councillors, (*Kungl. Maj:ts Kansli,* the Royal Chancellery; cf. "Administration") and a number of separate boards or government offices, each headed by a high officer from the civil service, a director general (*centrala ämbetsverk*, Central Administrative Boards).

The central administrative boards are of old standing in the national administration and have a number of characteristics peculiar to Sweden. They are staffed by a corps of civil servants who are appointed by the government, not elected to their posts. With the exception of the top officials, they enjoy permanent tenure, but even in the case of the former removal actually never occurs. Within their own spheres the boards are in a sense autonomous and make their own decisions. Their independent authority is delimited in by-laws issued by the King in Council. They are not directly responsible to any individual minister but rather to the existing laws; they are not part of the departments. Only the King in Council, as a body, can reverse the decision of such board. Opinions requested from the boards on a government proposal are made public and may be used to defeat the measure in question. In some respects this independence of the civil service is diminishing but is still important. Civil servants are eligible for Parliament and have full freedom of speech and vote in respect to the government in power.

These men and women, from the newest clerk to the director general, carry on the routine work of government and are responsible for translating the decisions of Cabinet and Parliament into action. While, for example, the Minister of Social Affairs determines policy, proposes legislation, and supervises social welfare throughout the nation, the personnel of such agencies as the Royal Social Board do the actual work of enforcing the letter and the spirit of the law. Civil servants work under the direction of cabinet ministers but are, as indicated above, in the end responsible to the laws, not to men.

As an interesting illustration of tradition in a government bureau an opinion handed down in 1926 by the Board of Exchequer *(Kammarkollegium)* may be cited. It stated that "the Court finds no cause to depart from its opinion as humbly represented to Your Majesty in 1697."

Local Government

Another administrative aspect of far-reaching importance is the extensive local autonomy, which likewise dates back to ancient times. The present division into townships, or communes, evolved from the early medieval parishes, each of which had as its center the local church and the "church village." Less directly the communes go back to the local things, popular assemblies at which the citizens met even earlier to deliberate and decide upon matters of common concern.

The parish, in turn, was composed of several villages, each with a board or council. In the parish council the villages found collective expression for their desires regarding the problems of the parish as a whole and the parish church. These administrative bodies passed through periods of varying importance; one major field was the care of the poor which the councils assumed in the eighteenth century.

As modern society evolved, the communes were assigned more numerous and important functions. In the middle of the last century the public elementary schools *(folkskolor)* were established and new laws for local self-government were passed, laws which became doubly important when the communal elections were made the basis for choosing representatives to the Upper House of Parliament. Originally all issues were settled by arriving at a consensus or a compromise. From the 1860's on, the local councils used a voting system based on property; in 1918 universal and equal suffrage was introduced.

Various local agencies manage poor relief, child welfare, unemployment problems, health and sanitation, building and construction, education, fire and police protection, and, in general, all communal functions. The local units have the right to tax themselves and thus provide the necessary funds. Issues within the sphere of other authorities, such as the national government, are carefully separated from those of the local bodies, but within almost every phase of their administration they carry out functions on behalf of the government. Additions to these can be made only by national legislation.

One somewhat problematic aspect of this autonomy is the variation in the economic resources of the communes.

The church parishes, each of which usually is an administrative unit in the rural areas, have remained essentially the same as in the early Middle Ages, when the recently Christianized inhabitants of a neighborhood banded together to build and support a church. In rich agricultural districts, where fewer people were required for the financing, the churches were many and the parishes small. Consequently, the communes of today in these areas (Skåne, Västergötland, Östergötland, and Gotland) are generally very small and include only a few hundred inhabitants. By contrast, some communes in the sparsely settled regions, particularly in the north, have a population of as many as 10 000, and in a few cases even more.

The differences in income level are sometimes quite large and are reflected in the local tax rates. The government attempts to ease the tax burden of certain hard-pressed communities by means of general grants-in-aid. The small units are frequently inefficient and inconvenient, but ancient and fiercely cherished traditions have made reorganization difficult. The opposition has finally given way, however, and the 1946 Parliament approved a proposal to merge the small parishes into larger units of at least 2 000 persons; units with less than 2 000 inhabitants are to be retained only in very exceptional cases.

The reorganization is to be completed by 1951, and should expedite considerably the work on social problems.

This aspect of local self-government and the problems involved has been the subject of much and lively public discussion, but there is no doubt about the great importance of autonomy as such. It enables men and women in towns as well as in the country to make significant contributions in public life. Every citizen is duty bound to perform conscientiously the functions entrusted to him in the elections. Frequently this kind of work has been the training school for those active in the political life of the nation.

Members of Parliament have often attained to their posts after having served their apprenticeship in the local administrations. The common efforts to serve the needs of the local unit across party lines have furthered objectivity and thoroughness. Thus thousands of men and women all over the country, who with honesty and devotion carry on their offices of trust, have become exponents of the very best in Swedish traditions. However, the increase in the amount of work required has made it more and more necessary, especially in cities and in the larger local units, to entrust the public tasks to paid officials.

Problems and functions which involve more than one commune, such as hospital care, road maintenance, education, and so forth, are referred to the county assembly, an institution established in 1862, and elected by the same constituents as other self-governing local bodies. The larger cities are outside this organization and handle such issues independently. As already indicated, the county assemblies and the councils of the larger towns are also the electoral bodies which choose the members for the Upper House of Parliament.

It has been emphasized time and again in previous sections that the ancient legal traditions have exerted a great influence on the formation of modern Sweden. They are evidenced in the oldest legal sources, the provincial laws from the thirteenth and fourteenth centuries. In some of their aspects these laws go back to heathen times, but even the oldest document, the "Older Västgöta Code," is pervaded by Christian concepts. "Land shall with law be built" is a literal phrase from one of the laws, and six hundred years later a Swedish king considered these words modern and applicable enough to use as his official motto. In olden times the peasants assembled for their local things, one in each province. The proceedings were led by a "lawman," the foremost man in the province, who knew the body of law by heart and interpreted it. Judgment was passed by the assembled multitude, and the litigants themselves participated in the execution of the penalties.

Sweden's first national codes were established in the middle of the fourteenth century, one applying to the towns, the other to the rural districts. In the main, this body of laws remained valid until replaced by the Code of 1734. The latter has been praised as "a hymn to the social philosophy of freedom and equality which prevailed in Sweden and Finland long before the concepts of modern democracy had been formulated." The subsequent development is based on that code.

The kings made great contributions both to the enactment and the administration of laws. It became a Swedish custom to "go to the King" when troublesome and involved cases occurred. A special member of the king's council who held the ancient office of *drots* (Chief Justice) was charged with this phase of the national government. The Council, with or without the king as chairman, was the highest instance, "the only court of appeal" for decisions made by the local courts.

In the seventeenth century new Appellate Courts (*hovrätter*) were established which reviewed contested decisions of the District Courts (*häradsrätter*) and City Courts (*rådhusrätter*). The king's council, or cabinet, served as the court of highest appeal, and thereby the legal system attained three levels, or even four in a number of court cases. Toward the end of the eighteenth century a Supreme Court was created which replaced the king's council as the highest judicial body. At present there are six Appellate Courts, situated in Stockholm, Jönköping, Malmö, Umeå, Göteborg, and Sundsvall.

An interesting feature of the District Courts are the seven to nine laymen in each who are elected to serve as "jurors" (*nämndemän*) and quasi as judges; in the City Courts such a "jury" (*nämnd*) serves only in serious criminal cases. The jurors are paid their travelling expenses and a per diem fee but do not at present receive a salary. They are not jurymen in the Anglo-Saxon sense but rather assistants to the judge, supplying him with information about litigants, witnesses, and local conditions which may have a bearing on the case. A majority of seven jurors out of the eight or nine present can determine the judgment or override the judge, but it seldom occurs. Regular juries are used, however, in press trials.

In addition to the legal system described above there are a number of special courts and tribunals, such as the Supreme Administrative Court (*Regeringsrätten*), dealing with appeals on questions in administration law, a special court on water rights, another concerned with land partitioning, police courts in the larger cities, and so forth.

Those without means are now entitled to legal process without court costs, and public legal-aid institutions set up by the local authorities assist those who cannot afford representation in court. Parliament also appoints two special High Commissioners as supervisors of civil and military administration, *Justitieombudsmannen,* (JO) and *Militieombudsmannen,* (MO) respectively to make certain that the laws and the rights of individuals are conscientiously observed by all officials. Any citizen may turn to these commissioners "to complain about conditions within the administration which he does not consider in accord with what is right and reasonable."

Time-honored phrases are echoed in the paragraph from the Constitution Act of 1809 which states the legal heritage in condensed form and has justly been called the Magna Charta of Swedish freedom:

"The King shall strengthen and promote justice and truth, prevent and prohibit wrongs and injustice; neither destroy nor tolerate the destruction of anyone's life, honor, personal freedom, or general welfare, except by legal conviction and sentence; nor shall he deprive anyone, or allow that anyone be deprived of any property, real or movable, without due process and judgment in accordance with the laws and statutes of Sweden; nor shall he violate or allow the violation of anyone's peace in his home; nor banish anyone from one place to another; nor shall he coerce or allow the coercion of anyone's conscience, but shall protect each and every one in the free exercise of his religion, insofar as the public peace is not disturbed or general offense caused. The King shall allow everyone to be judged by the court to which he legally is subject."

POLITICAL PARTIES

In the Era of Liberty the Hats and Caps (page 137) created with their bitter feuds a lasting popular aversion toward party

170

politics. Nevertheless, such activity was defended in the eighteenth century by the traveled Swedish poet Jacob Wallenberg, who drew some international parallels in the following stanza:

"Let Hats and Caps fight on, let discord's thunder rumble:
An oak which now and then is shaken by a blast
      Below the ground holds firm and fast.
When Rome its squabbles ceased she had begun to tumble,
And England gains her peak admidst dispute and strife.
      Free states from party feuds draw life."

But the memory of the misadventures in foreign affairs during the eighteenth century persisted. When the Hats and Caps retired from the stage and a new party system was in formation, this too was looked upon with definite, though gradually abating mistrust. A two-party system continued as long as the four estates existed in Parliament; the Hats and Caps had their parallels in the Conservatives and Liberals, respectively, toward the middle of the nineteenth century. Only with the establishment of the bicameral parliament did the modern party system make its groping debut in Swedish politics.

Since that time the parties have suffered many changes. At present there are five: Conservatives *(högern)*, Farmers' Union *(bondeförbundet)*, People's Party or Liberals *(folkpartiet)*, Social Democrats, and Communists.

In giving a thumbnail sketch of each party, the Conservatives may be said to live up to their name fairly well but have recently become more receptive to reform proposals. They consider private ownership and enterprise a prerequisite to sound progress. State employees, businessmen, and farmers account for an appreciable share of the Conservative Party membership.

The Farmers' Union was started to further the interests of the rural districts, which are claimed to be neglected in comparison with those of the towns. Occasionally this party will put up candidates in a town election, but its members are primarily farmers.

The People's Party draws most of its adherents from the temperance movement and the nonconformist groups but also has a considerable following within other sections of the "middle class" and among the small farmers. Furthermore, a number of the leading industrialists, not to mention a large group of the intellectuals, belong to this party. The Liberals are fervent advocates of social reforms, champion civil liberties, and resist the continuing expansion of the government's business enterprises.

The Social Democrats, Sweden's labor party, are nowadays perhaps more cautious in favoring reforms—in order to gain more distribution of wealth—and have retained less of the socialist tinge than the emphasis in the party name indicates. Most of their adherents are industrial workers and employees in other economic fields, largely members of the trade unions. Gradually the party has also gained support among the "radical" elements of the normally conservative state employees and in academic circles. The party has professed to be "identical with social democracy in other countries" thus indicating more than a national philosophy in its tenets. Its "Twenty-seven Points," a postwar program, have found support even among the Communists, which, however, does not imply any great degree of compatability between the two parties.

The Communists are, of course, strict Marxists and count their supporters mainly in the large cities and among the workers in the industrial sections of Norrland. The small nazi-tinged groups, which never gained enough support to be represented in Parliament, have now disappeared almost entirely.

In this connection a mention should be made of the leading party personalities. Admiral Arvid Lindman (1862—1936), can in the main be considered the creator of the modern Conservative Party. The founder of the modern Liberal Party and an energetic champion of parliamentarism in the early twentieth century was Karl Staaff (1860—1915), by profession a lawyer. Hjalmar Branting (1860—1925), an intellectual and originally a newspaper editor, remains a venerated figure in the Social Democratic Labor Party, to which he gave outstanding leadership from the 1890's until his death in 1925. His work was continued by Per Albin Hansson, the prime minister who died in 1946. Hansson too was a newspaperman and guided the country's destiny for fourteen years. His successor is Tage Erlander, a young intellectual who has risen rapidly to the premiership through various stages in government service. The leader of the Farmers' Union, Axel Pehrsson-Bramstorp, is himself a farmer and headed the "Hundred Day Government" which made the only brief break in P. A. Hansson's regime. The People's Party is led by Bertil Ohlin, a professor of economics; the Conservatives by Fritiof Domö, a landowner; and the Communists by Sven Linderot, a newspaperman.

Parliament's political center of gravity lies in the Lower House, of which the party leaders as a rule are members. Party affiliations are indicated for both chambers in the table below; the figures for 1944 have been included to indicate the trend during the four-year period.

Another view of party relations and shifts is obtained from the list of cabinets since 1917 given below. It should be noted, however, that most of the earlier ones on the list were minority cabinets. The country was stable enough but the political

173

Parties	Members of Parliament				Votes cast in election of	
	Upper House		Lower House		1944	1948
	1944	1948	1944	1948		
Conservatives	26	25	39	23	488 921	478 779
Farmers' Union....	21	21	35	30	421 094	480 360
People's Party.....	14	16	26	57	398 293	882 414
Social Democrats ..	86	85	115	112	1 436 571	1 789 440
Communists	3	3	15	8	318 466	244 812
Total	150	150	230	230	3 063 345	3 875 805

balance so sensitive that is was often necessary to juggle the party groups and govern with "shifting majorities."

Prime Minister	Cabinet	Period of Office
Nils Edén	Liberal-Social Democrats	1917—1920
Hjalmar Branting	Social Democrats	March—October 1920
Louis de Geer	Administrative	1920—1921
Oscar Fredrik von Sydow	Administrative	Febr.—Oct. 1921
Hjalmar Branting	Social Democrats	1921—1923
Ernst Trygger	Conservatives	1923—1924
Hjalmar Branting (d. 1925) Rickard Sandler	Social Democrats	1924—1926
Carl Gustaf Ekman	People's Party	1926—1928
Arvid Lindman	Conservatives	1928—1930
Carl Gustaf Ekman Felix Hamrin (last two months)	People's Party	1930—1932
Per Albin Hansson	Social Democrats	1932—1936

Axel Pehrsson-Brams-torp	Farmers' Union	Summer, 1936
Per Albin Hansson	Social Democrats and Farmers' Union	1936—1939
Per Albin Hansson	All-party Coalition, except Communists	1939—1945
Per Albin Hansson (d. 1946) Tage Erlander	Social Democrats	1945—

In the general elections of 1944 there were more than four million voters, of whom 71.9 % went to the polls. This percentage had been surpassed only once; in the 1936 elections 74.5 % cast their ballots. In 1948, however, there were 300 000 voters more than in 1944 and a record number (83 %) went to the polls.

THE PRESS

For a century and more the Swedish press has been independent of the state in the sense that anyone has the right to publish a newspaper, that censorship is forbidden, and that the publication of a newspaper cannot be prohibited by law. The statutes contained in Swedish law which provide penalties for certain utterances, such as sacrilege, libel of government authorities, and statements offensive to public morality, have repeatedly been modified and given an increasingly lenient interpretation. In recent times the freedom of the press has generally been looked upon as an indispensable component of democracy. No attempts at restriction have been made as a result of state policy. It can without any hesitation be claimed that this civic freedom is as complete and as well protected in Sweden as in any other democracy.

175

Departures from the general trend of this development were in evidence only during the second world war. The freedom of the press was restricted in some respects, mainly and without doubt because of pressure from Berlin. Especially notable was the fact that in a large number of cases the government revived a statute which previously had been considered defunct. It was used to confiscate newspapers which contained attacks of an allegedly derogatory nature on the German leaders and authorities. However, the confiscations applied only to the issue or issues containing such attacks. Prohibition to publish a newspaper could not be enacted, and a censorship was not introduced, even though a constitutional change was made to pave the way for censorship regulations in case of war or imminent danger of war. The steps taken in the face of the German threat caused opposition in press and parliament, and they were retracted even before the end of the European war. It should be emphatically underscored here that the restrictions of the freedom of the press never went so far as to prevent a criticism of Germany and her government, as long as it was held within somewhat moderate bounds. In this connection it is of interest to note that the English propaganda sheet *News from Great Britain* was published in Swedish throughout the war and distributed in hundreds of thousands of copies.

According to all indications, the press of the Scandinavian countries has made extraordinarily rapid progress in our own times, especially during recent years. The newspapers have added more and more pages, many of them as a result of increased advertising. Instead of four or eight pages half a century ago, they now carry 20—30. However, the number of pages has been reduced since World War II because of the paper rationing. In circulation the increase has been tremendous. This was particularly notable during the last war, and the number of readers then obtained has remained fairly constant. From 1942 to 1948 the total net circulation of papers issued at least twice a week in Sweden rose from 2 486 900 copies to 3 235 400, an increase of 30 %. A number of the larger papers have doubled their circulation many times over in recent decades. *Dagens Nyheter,* at present the largest paper in Sweden, went from 25 000 copies in 1909 to 242 000 in 1948.

Some aspects of the papers appearing two or more times a week are shown in the following table. It should be emphasized, however, that the papers appearing daily or six times weekly dominate overwhelmingly in circulation. The table includes statistics covering the number of papers, their total net circulation, and party affiliation: furthermore, the number of papers and total circulation ascribable to each political party are reduced to percentages, and, finally, the percentage of voters for the party in question at the most recent election.

Swedish Newspapers 1948, first half of the year

Party	Number of Papers	Circulation	%	Percentage of Votes 1948
Conservatives	82	738 700	22.8	12.3
Farmers' Union	21	149 400	4.6	12.4
People's Party	62	1 590 700	49.2	22.7
Social Democrats	35	536 500	16.6	46.2
Communists	3	56 000	1.7	6.3
Non-politicals	36	164 100	5.1	0.1
Total	239	3 235 400	100.0	100.0

The average is one paper for every two inhabitants, indicating that almost all families subscribe to a paper and that many buy two or more.

A notable feature in Sweden, as in all the Scandinavian countries, is the important position held by the press of the

177

capital. The big Stockholm papers can be quickly distributed throughout the country, and they are correctly referred to as "national newspapers." Their circulation is an impressive 1 010 200, or 37 % of the total, if papers published less than six times a week are excluded. Even in other countries—England, Belgium, Holland, France—the concentration of the newspapers in the capital or the largest cities is striking. The outstanding papers in these cities can be called national in the sense that they are sold all over the country. In the United States, on the other hand, hardly any paper could be called national in this sense. This is a natural consequence of the country's tremendous size, and hence the circulation of the large American papers is proportionately lower than that in the smaller European countries.

A comparison between the circulation of the papers affiliated with the various parties and their respective number of votes in the elections gives interesting results. In regard to circulation, the party papers that may be said to represent conservative and liberal opinions are, on the whole, far ahead of the number of their adherents among the voters. Their share in circulation is almost 72 %, while their percentage of voters is only 35. This difference is most striking in the case of the liberal People's Party: the circulation of its press is 49.2 %, but its share at the polls only 22.7 %. The Social Democrats, Communists, and the Farmers' Union, on the other hand, have a relatively small representation in newspapers.

To a large extent the "overrepresentation" in the press of certain parties is ascribable to their having larger papers than the others, i. e. the differences among the parties apply primarily to circulation, not to the number of papers published. The Social Democratic papers in Sweden are of average size, but the People's Party especially is represented by newspapers with exceptionally large circulation.

178

In these respects the Scandinavian press does not to any remarkable extent differ from that of other countries. For instance, in 1947 the United States had 1 740 newspapers with a total circulation of more than 50 millions, i. e. in proportion to the population somewhat fewer papers but about the same circulation. A similar situation is found in most European countries, except in England, where there are relatively few papers with exceptionally large circulation. In non-Scandinavian countries, like in Sweden, the Socialist and Communist press seems as a rule to be weaker than the number of voters for the respective parties would indicate.

In respect to ownership it may be said that the non-socialist papers, excepting some of those adhering to the Farmers' Union, are in the hands of publishing companies or individual owners, a fact especially true of the large non-socialist papers. However, the papers in this category are in some cases owned by organizations, mostly political, or occasionally by foundations established to guarantee the existence of the newspaper in question and assure its independence. What is thus generally true of the non-socialist press is the exception among the Social Democrat and Communist newspapers. In Sweden, as in the other northern countries, they are almost exclusively established by the party or its affiliated organizations, primarily those of the labor movement. Consequently, these papers are, essentially, the organs of a political party, their chief aim being to carry on propaganda for this party.

From the foregoing it is evident that when a given paper is called liberal, another social democratic, their affiliation with the respective party may frequently be entirely different in nature. A number of the non-socialist newspapers are first and foremost directed toward news coverage, information, and leisure reading. The party affiliation merely means that in general, and especially at election time, they support their party, while the leftist papers are much more constantly aligned for political work.

Thus the non-socialist press is largely independent in its relation to party leadership and organizations. But what is the position of the paper, or rather its editor-in-chief, to the owners? In many cases, especially those of smaller papers, this problem does not exist, since the owner and the editor are one and the same person; a number of Swedish journalists have at an early age started work with a newspaper which they have gradually taken over and have now been identified with for decades. The problem is of importance especially in the case of the larger newspapers, owned either by companies or by individuals who are not engaged, at least not primarily, in work on the paper and do not in any case write for it. In this connection certain tendencies have lately become particularly evident in England and the United States which are generally looked upon as undesirable. A concern, sometimes dominated by a single individual, owns a chain of newspapers which are centrally managed and whose editors must in effect write according to given directions. It is unlikely that such a situation would be paralleled in the Swedish press, where it is taken for granted throughout that the editor-in-chief is the real head of the paper.

In Stockholm the Social Democratic views are expressed in *Morgon-Tidningen,* those of the People's Party, though with varying slants, in *Dagens Nyheter, Stockholms-Tidningen,* and *Svenska Morgonbladet.* The Conservatives are represented by *Svenska Dagbladet* and the Communists by *Ny Dag.* All of these are morning papers. There are three afternoon papers: *Aftonbladet* and *Expressen* are largely mouthpieces of the People's Party; *Afton-Tidningen* is Social Democratic, supported by the trade unions. The Farmers' Union has no leading paper such as those of other parties in the capital, which is understandable enough in view of its membership, but *Skånska Dagbladet*, published in Malmö, is considered its standard-bearer.

One of the newspapers published outside the capital, the *Göteborgs Handels- och Sjöfartstidning* (People's Party), has already been mentioned in another connection. *Göteborgs-Posten*, also a People's Party organ, vies with *Dagens Nyheter* for the largest circulation among the country's newspapers. Another leading paper of the Social Democrats, *Ny Tid*, is published in Göteborg, a third, *Arbetet*, in Malmö. The latter city is also the home of the great Conservative newspaper *Sydsvenska Dagbladet Snällposten*. Sparsely populated Norrland also boasts several good newspapers. The largest are *Västerbottens-Kuriren* in Umeå and *Sundsvalls Tidning* in Sundsvall, (People's Party), *Östersunds-Posten* in Östersund (Conservatives), and *Norrländska Socialdemokraten* in Boden. The only bilingual paper is *Haparanda-bladet*, which is also printed in Finnish on account of the large population element speaking that language in the nearby boundary regions.

The political debate is largely confined to the press. Reports on the deliberations in Parliament are constantly decreasing in importance, mainly because those on more vital issues would merely repeat views and arguments already aired in the press. Speeches and other political activities reach a larger public by being carried or reported on in the papers. Only the radio with its lectures and debates is comparable to the press in these respects, but in the northern countries it has been relatively little utilized as a political instrument, so that the position of the press has not been seriously affected.

An important fact is that the discussions carried on among the papers from various political camps are particularly lively in Scandinavia. Especially in Norway and Sweden, other newspapers are regularly quoted as part of the news coverage, then commended or criticized. A not inconsiderable part of the editorials is devoted to polemics with other papers; in the smaller towns where two newsorgans with diametrically opposed political views may struggle for dominance, such polemics occasionally assume unreasonably large proportions. On the whole, however, this constant battle among the papers is undoubtedly an important factor in maintaining the public's interest in politics and in giving the citizenry a knowledge of the significant differences in opinion. The tone in these debates has become sharper in recent years—particularly in Sweden since the formation of a wholly Social Democratic cabinet in 1945—but it is incomparably more objective and polite than it was a few decades ago.

In addition to the newspapers Sweden has, of course, weekly news and pictorial magazines, learned and professional journals, and periodicals dealing with industry and business in their various aspects. However, in the public debates not at least in the cultural field the newspapers play a far greater role than the periodicals, which on the whole are insignificant, aside from the numerous publications for light reading and amusement.

SOCIAL WELFARE, EDUCATION, AND POPULAR MOVEMENTS

ENLIGHTENED DEMOCRACY

SOCIAL WELFARE

EDUCATION

POPULAR MOVEMENTS

SPORTS AND GYMNASTICS

ENLIGHTENED DEMOCRACY

Greater knowledge and more extensive schooling are prerequisite for a vigorous and alert democracy in which the people examine issues and express opinions, going to the polls, as it were, every day. "He who will may try before he judges" is a pithy line from Esaias Tegnér, one of Sweden's classic poets. An essential objective of democracy is to give every man and woman the opportunity to "try" the issues, weigh them intelligently, and form independent conclusions without interference or influence from other quarters.

Public issues become a part of the people themselves if they feel that as citizens they are personally concerned in each, a feeling developed by proper education and training in analytical, independent judgment. These are the principles that form the background of social welfare, education, and general social activities in Sweden.

SOCIAL WELFARE

Swedish progress in social security has received flattering attention from abroad. Generous observers from England have compared Sweden's measures favorably with those of New

Zealand and Australia; Americans have been free with their praises and to an extent consider Sweden both a model country and a proving ground for social reforms. When considering such comparisons and appraisals it should be remembered that Sweden has had much more time for social development than Australia or New Zealand and that in Sweden the scale is smaller, conditions more uniform, the population more homogeneous than in the United States.

Some of the fundamental principles in Sweden's social legislation can be traced back a couple of centuries. Beginning in 1763, each parish was required to care for its own aged, infirm, and otherwise needy people, the costs to be covered by local taxation. The debate concerning this type of poor relief was particularly intensive in the early part of the nineteenth century when a part of the agrarian population was becoming pauperized. The pros and cons of the problem engaged some of the best minds in the country.

Today's efforts are directed more and more toward erasing the old concept of poor relief. Social insurance is the advocated replacement. Preventive aid is considered most effective; society is to give its needy "help to help themselves." This trend has been accelerated as a result of the industrialization, which brought in its wake a number of new problems, such as those concerned with working hours, child labor, women workers, industrial safety, the right of workers to organize and bargain collectively.

Some of these issues were faced as early as the 1880's, but the sociopolitical controversies and reforms did not gather real momentum until after the turn of the century. When the suffrage was extended in 1907—1909, the path was cleared for general old age and invalidity pensions as well as protective laws for labor.

Foreign visitors frequently ask in what situations or emergencies a Swedish citizen benefits from the social reforms achieved so far. Perhaps the clearest answer results from tracing a lifespan and its normal exigencies.

About 95 % of the mothers receive assistance at the birth of their children in the form of maternity benefits paid jointly by hospitalization plans and the government. In addition, a needy mother may receive further allowances upon investigation of her case. A total of more than twenty-four million dollars has been disbursed during the last ten years, making childbirth practically cost free and also providing certain clothing and supplies for the newborn. Maternity and pediatric centers have been established which give free consultations and examinations to women in connection with pregnancy and to preschool children. School-age children are examined twice yearly by the school physician free of charge. Dental care in the schools is becoming increasingly common. In Stockholm this work is given outstanding aid by the Eastman Institute, a model dental clinic established through the generosity of the American philanthropist George Eastman.

Families with many children enjoy certain privileges and exemptions; for example, recently a facility allowance system was introduced, granting a cash payment for each child under sixteen, regardless of income, amounting to about $ 73 a year. This plan went into effect during the first quarter of 1948. Orphans, fatherless children, and children of invalid parents receive state benefits.

Free school lunches have been a feature of the school system in some parts of Sweden for quite a while, but in general they have provided only for needy children. Arrangements have now been made to give all children in school a free noonday meal, and steady progress is made in the realization of this plan as additional facilities are secured.

Almost all children under fourteen are entitled by statute

one free roundtrip journey for vacation purposes. Vacation camps are also supported by the government. Mothers may accompany children under ten free of charge. Meanwhile, in order to make it easier for housewives with several children to take holidays, they have also been granted free travel to and from a vacation spot. Mothers with two or more minor children living at home are eligible, if under a certain income level, and can generally be away from home for at least ten days.

Still another vacation-for-housewives project has now been launched in the form of inexpensive holidays at adult education centers and other institutions.

In this connection the domestic aid plan is also of interest. This service is designed to relieve the critical situation that arises when the mother of small children is temporarily incapacitated. A trained home assistant is sent to take charge of the household during the emergency, replacing or assisting the housewife in the care of home and family, particularly the children. In 1948 the government granted funds sufficient to maintain a staff of 2 500 such assistants.

It is an old tradition in Sweden that both health and illness are matters of public concern. The district assemblies *(landsting)* are charged with the conduct and maintenance of district hospitals, tuberculosis sanatoria, and hospitals for contagious diseases. This responsibility became law in 1931 and is now alleviated by financial aid from the state amounting to about one half of the cost. The extent of the public health services is indicated by the fact that less than three percent of the nation's hospital beds are in private institutions. Dental care for the entire population is also being organized in accordance with a plan adopted in 1938, the basic provision of which is a corps of regional dentists engaged by the district assemblies and the larger cities.

The sum of all these provisions and many others too numerous for mention is that the cost of good health and care when ill is very low. District hospital ward rates have been figured at 50—75 cents a day, dropping to one half of that after thirty days; in Stockholm the ward rate is around $ 1.37, reduced to 88 cents after fifteen days. Even this small expense is normally covered by the individual's group insurance.

Periodic physical examinations are becoming more and more widespread; fluoroscopy is employed for early detection of the dreaded tuberculosis. In every possible way the authorities work on keeping people well rather than restoring their health. Consequently, public health officials are also deeply concerned with the regulation of housing in accordance with the demands of hygiene and sanitation. A decided need exists here, for the housing standard is still too low. In Sweden's northerly climate, housing has to be solid. Heating costs are high—even as far south as Stockholm, heat is required two-thirds of the year.

All this makes housing expensive—and living space is often cramped. If crowded housing is defined as the accommodation of more than two people in each room, excluding the kitchen, 28 % of the housing and 38 % of the inhabitants are crowded. Until recently, the most marketable apartment consisted of one room and kitchen, and even larger apartments did not provide adequate space for families with children. It is therefore not surprising that the housing problem is very much in the limelight. During the war new construction lagged since both manpower and industry were engaged in the defense effort and food production. Realization of the postwar plans for prompt remedy has been delayed by shortage of both labor and material. Brisk building activity is, nevertheless, going on within the limits of the resources.

Government subsidies during the last five years have reduced the ratio of one-room apartments in new buildings from 40 to 20 per cent, and the over-all space has increased by at least 25 per cent in these structures.

Organized government and municipal aid, together with prefabrication, have made home ownership a possibility even in low income groups. A man may pay for his house over a twenty-year period at a lower annual outlay than he would have to pay in rent for a city apartment, provided he does the erecting or corresponding construction work himself.

Cooperative ownership of apartments is also widespread. HSB, a nation-wide organization which acts as contractor and central accounting office for individual groups building apartments, sponsors about one tenth of all the dwelling units built in Sweden today. Owner investment (5—10 per cent) brings down annual amortization, which is payable as rent.

Housing for the workers in Sweden's decentralized industries has largely had to be provided by the companies themselves, either by direct building, or in affiliation with the government-subsidized home ownership and cooperative systems.

Since the war governmental subsidies have been granted in order to maintain the actual cost of housing at the pre-war level. Additional subsidies are forthcoming in favor of families with at least two children or low income. Government mortgage terms favor cooperative and municipal financing, but private enterprise has provided most of the housing to date.

Some of the experiments with various types of settlements, including housing specifically designed for families with several children, actually classify among the government's efforts to increase the birth rate, which between the world wars sank to a precariously low point. The population problem became one of the most serious, and many of the social measures since the mid-30's should be viewed against that background. Previous mention has been made of the relatively high living standard. Some of that standard was acquired at the cost of a lower birth rate. During the first five years of the present century 26.12 children were born annually per thousand inhabitants, while during 1931—1935 the corresponding figure was only 14.10. This had risen to 19.6 in 1946, in which year the United States rate was 23.3. Swedish sociologists predict that as a consequence the present manpower shortage will remain acute until about the mid-60's.

Education, usually the child's first major departure from home life and parents, will be dealt with in the next section of this chapter. Beyond that he faces work opportunities and working conditions. The assumption is that our chosen life-span is that of a normal person of good habits and in no need of special care, such as that given to alcoholics or asocial individuals.

Vocational guidance is becoming increasingly available and young people are advised not merely to enter fields that have openings for newcomers but to choose those most suitable for each individual. However, Sweden has not advanced so far in this work as some other countries, notably the United States. The State Employment Board maintains offices and provides free employment service in all administrative districts and larger cities. Their obvious task is to secure for the employer the best qualified workers, for the employee the job best suited to his training and talents. This service handles about one million placements annually, but in recent years the labor supply has not been able to meet the demand.

An eight-hour law for industrial workers was passed in 1919, for farm workers in 1936, and for business employees in 1939. Statutory vacations for wage earners have also been introduced and guarantee a minimum of one day for each month of employment, or twelve days annually (for workers under 18 years eighteen days). Laws for the protection of workers against occupation hazards have been considerably broadened and include protective regulations applying to minors and women workers. State safety inspectors make certain that the provisions are followed; the workers themselves also elect a safety representative in factories with more than ten workers, on the large farms, and in other concerns. Workmen's industrial accident insurance is compulsory and paid entirely by the employers.

Adequate provisions for illness have not yet gone into effect. The health insurance or sick benefit organizations that exist are, however, recognized by the government, and about 60 % of the adult population are members of such groups. Late in 1946 Parliament passed a compulsory sickness insurance law providing for medical care and cash allowances but because of budget considerations it probably will not begin to operate until 1951. When the new system goes into effect, the hospitalization plan and health insurance will be two separate and distinct fields. Under the former, every Swedish citizen will be entitled to free treatment in public hospitals. Certain basic medicines will be dispensed free, others at half price upon presentation of a doctor's prescription. These services will be paid for by the government and will have no relation to the health insurance system.

The health insurance associations will pay three fourths of the physician's fee, as stipulated in the law, all travel expenses of the patient, and a daily compensation during the period of his illness. The patient will be able freely to choose his doctor. As it now stands, the associations pay two thirds of the doctor's bill, two thirds of the hospital costs, and a daily compensation.

Many Swedish planners hope that unemployment insurance will also become obligatory within the near future. Steps taken in the past to relieve long periods of unemployment were

74 and 75. Modern housing architecture in Sweden has set the pace in planning for space and light around living quarters in the city. Playgrounds and recreational opportunities for the small children are standard features. Modern quarters in Stockholm at Tessin Park and Norr Mälarstrand. Photos by C. G. Rosenberg.

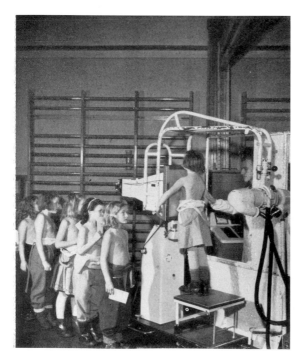

76 and 77. The upper picture shows the Eastman Institute in Stockholm, where free dental care is given thousands of children. Left: Fluoroscopy in a primary school in Stockholm. This type of examination is now obligatory in all Swedish schools. Photos by Herman Rönninger and Bo Törngren.

78 and 79. South Hospital (*Södersjukhuset*) in Stockholm is one of the world's most modern in its provisions for treatment and its technical equipment. Above: The new South Hospital and, right, a lounge for convalescent patients. Photos by Gösta Lundquist and Bo Törngren.

80. Public libraries with free loan privileges are found throughout Sweden. A view from the City Library in Stockholm. Photo by K. W. Gullers.

81. Swedish children of today receive their instruction in well lighted schools with modern equipment. Eriksdalsskolorna in Stockholm. Photo by Andreas Feininger.

82. Sports and life in the open occupy a considerable share of Swedish leisure time. In the summer long bicycle trips are popular, especially among the young people. The many youth hostels and the ever-present cycle provide good opportunities for young and old to become acquainted with their native land. Swedish girl at a youth hostel. Photo by Gösta Lundquist.

83 and 84. The great forests and numerous waterways provide vacation spots with wonderful recreational possibilities in all seasons. Winter forest in Dalarna, and canoeing on a forest stream in Norrland. Photos by Anders Erkers and Gösta Lundquist.

85, 86, and 87. One part or the other of Sweden's extensive shoreline is the goal of vacationing people throughout the summer. Bathing on the rocky Bohuslän shore. Photo by K. W. Gullers. — Taking long trips in the winter and live in self-made igloos is a more strenuous form of outdoor life, but in summer the northern mountains attract even those who are not too adventurous. On the oposite page, below: Igloo occupants in the Sarek Mountains, Lappland, and, above, a valley scene near Kebnekaise, Lappland. Photos by Sven Öman and Georg Bergwall.

88 and 89. Outdoor sports, among them skiing, have many followers in Sweden. Two Olympic gold medal winners in action. At top, Henry Ericsson, winner of the 1,500 meter race at the London Olympics, and, left, Nils Karlsson, winner of the 50 kilometer ski run in S:t Moritz. Photos by Text & Bilder and A. Hörnell.

90. Sweden's most popular game is soccer. Every Sunday in spring and autumn it attracts large crowds of spectators all over the country. The gold medal in the Olympic soccer tournament of 1948 was won by the Swedish team. Soccer match in the Råsunda Stadium, Stockholm. Photo by Text & Bilder.

91. Swedish gymnastics enjoy a far-flung reputation. On exhibition tours in England and the United States Sweden's women gymnasts have won acclamation for their grace and rhythmic skill. The Sofia Girls in action. Photo by Text & Bilder.

improvised to meet each situation. Available at present are unemployment insurance societies which can help the worker survive a relatively brief period without work. Any qualified organization of workers (usually, but not necessarily connected a labor union) will receive state contributions to its unemployment insurance fund, in which the employers do not participate as, for instance, in the United States. In 1948 the members numbered about 1 020 400.

Thus the major crises in man's active life are met by more or less adequate provisions. What happens in old age or in case of disability? A law was passed in 1913 which provided old age and disability insurance for the entire population. This "people's pension law," as it is called, has since been improved several times and a new change went into effect on January 1, 1948. The annual premiums paid by everyone not a beneficiary under the plan range from $ 1.68 to $ 28.00, depending on income. All citizens receive a basic pension when attaining the age of 67 or when becoming unable to work before that age. This amounts to $ 280.00 a year ($ 448.00 for married couples) and will be increased by "rent allowances" ranging from $ 42.00—$ 168.00 ($ 56.00—$ 224.00 for married couples) annually, depending on locality and other sources of income. Furthermore, certain local grants are also available. This new reform, which will cost the government an additional $ 112 million yearly, has appreciably increased the modest pensions previously paid and will, besides, encourage savings and employment past the pension age limit. It provides for no affluent living but enables everyone to "get along."

The attempts on the part of the state to give its citizens help to help themselves "from womb to tomb" — as the English put it — give all possible support and stability to their work and intercede when they are faced with adversity. Ordinary poor relief, which preventive social planning hopes to abolish, still exists in addition to the welfare system traced above.

The whole population problem is at present the subject of an inclusive survey and remains one of the focal points in the home policy. All parties are in agreement on the principles; the controversies deal with what the nation can afford, which reforms should be given priority, and how speedily they should be carried through. The social provisions for the support and protection of children and young people hold a central place in the theory and practice of Swedish social welfare. They are based on three basic principles: the realization that the nation's human material is its most valuable asset; the endeavor to create greater equality of opportunity for all; and the concept that social assistance, wherever possible, be applied so as to prevent illness and waste of human energies and potentialities instead of merely patching up their consequences. Building healthy, happy generations and offering equal opportunities to the individuals are considered major steps toward these goals.

EDUCATION

In the areas of universities, schools, and adult education farreaching reforms are also in preparation, designed to give the citizenry increased knowledge and more training, extensive and intensive.

Sweden has only four universities, but they begin at a stage corresponding to the junior or senior college year in the United States and the studies lead only to advanced degrees. Two of these institutions, at Uppsala (founded 1477) and Lund (founded 1668), are state supported and fullfledged universities in the European sense, i. e. with faculties in theology, law, medicine, and philosophy (humanities and natural sciences). Stockholm University at present has faculties in law, humanities, and natural sciences. The Caroline Medical Institute, Sweden's chief institution for medical training and research, also in Stockholm, has full university rank in medicine and includes a large, modern hospital. In Lund, Stockholm, and Göteborg institutes are located for advanced studies in the social work and public administration to which qualified students are admitted whether secondary school (*läroverk*) graduates or not. Stockholm, furthermore, has a number of graduate schools in special fields, including those of forestry, commerce, dentistry, veterinary science, arts, music, pharmacy, technology, and so forth.

Göteborg University curricula are confined to the humanities. The city is also the seat of higher institutions for economic and technical studies, notably the Chalmer Institute of Technology, which in its upper division offers work leading to the doctor of engineering degree.

University studies in Sweden, at least in Uppsala and Lund, have sometimes been charged with being antiquated and steeped in traditionalism, but those two institutions have, on the other hand, been favorably compared by foreign observers with Oxford and Cambridge as distinguished seats of education and culture. Admittedly they need to be modernized, and a reform is now in preparation. In 1948 the students in the universities and other graduate schools numbered 14 000, of whom 3 250 were women. Since the last two years in the secondary school system are considered equivalent to the junior college course or the freshman and sophomore college years in the United States, the number of students in schools of higher learning, in the American sense, is considerably greater than the figures above indicate.

An important extension of university and research activities is in progress. Large sums have been reserved for scholarships, enlargement of the various research institutes, the acquisition of equipment, and so forth. On the whole the entire research and instruction program is being subjected to revision.

The primary and secondary school systems are even more than the universities under consideration for reform. Everyone's basic education is at present a seven-year course, ending normally at the age of fourteen, while in England eight years, in the United States ten to twelve years are devoted to the fundamental preparation. Some of Sweden's elementary schools already give a basic eight-year course, and either that or nine years are indicated as the future minimum.

The intermediate education is obtained in secondary schools (*läroverk*), which, however, like some preparatory schools in the United States, include the upper years of elementary work. In general, a nine-year course, including the elementary years, leads to the Lower Certificate (*realexamen*), a twelve-year course to the Diploma (*studentexamen*). The main subjects are modern foreign languages, humanities, natural science, and mathematics. Oral and written examinations for the Diploma are administered by the National Board of Education and must be passed for admission to university or other graduate school studies. About 4 000 candidates pass this *studentexamen* annually.

In sparsely populated areas where the schools are far apart, young people are still at a disadvantage in respect to advanced secondary and higher education. Many proposals for a solution have been and are under discussion. Meanwhile, education by correspondence makes a notable contribution by offering higher education to ambitious young people in isolated sections of the country, not to mention those with full programs of study pursued after working hours. In recent years the correspondence institutes, all of which are private, have convened full-course students in refresher seminars before they face their major examinations. Attempts are also made to combine instruction by correspondence and radio, as in the elementary foreign language courses, apparently an excellent device for providing audio-oral training and overcoming some of the disadvantages of living in areas far from the educational centers. Another valuable reform has brought increased possibilities to rural youths who wish to continue their studies in towns with more advanced educational institutions. A basic allowance of about $ 150 is guaranteed every qualified applicant whose continued studies necessitate travelling or living away from home. If such an applicant can pass a general test given to both local and out-of-town students with a rating above the average, he is entitled to a supplementary grant of about $ 140. In this way more than a thousand young people are enabled annually to proceed with their secondary education largely at the expense of the state.

All over the nation intensive interest is shown in building a modern, vital school system based on sound psychological principles. Vocational education has made rapid progress, especially in the population centers; here, too, fair and justified demands are made by the remote regions for more equal opportunities.

Free and independent self-education pursued by the Swedish people has attracted much attention abroad. Even in the most remote settlements men and women are found who have chosen intensive studies as their avocation. A small farmer, for example, has spent the spare time of his life in collecting the stone and bronze age relics found in his home parish, scientifically identifying and cataloguing them with the aid of books on the subject which he has procured. Another had made his native dialect the subject of painstaking study which in 1932 was rewarded by Uppsala University with its highest honor, the Ph. D. *honoris causa* degree. Some years ago an old shoemaker from the Närke countryside told radio listeners about his self-education; his ambition was to read the world's classics in the original tongues, and consequently he had acquired several foreign languages on his own to realize his goal. Such cases are, of course, exceptions, but interest in education is deep and sustained throughout the nation.

It was a fortunate day in the Swedish pursuit of knowledge when the popular movements and their leaders turned to education a few decades ago as a means of furthering their ideals. The results have been impressive, especially since the English study-circle method was adopted. By now a network of 15 000 study circles covers the country with a student body of almost 180 000. State subsidies make possible the scheduling of frequent public lectures (nearly 7 000 annually, average attendance over 100) on almost any desired subject in most communities.

In July, 1947, government subsidies for adult education work were considerably increased and now cover 50 per cent of the administrative costs. Specific grants make it possible for the associations to employ more full-time advisors and instructors to train more study-circle leaders and expand the lecture programs. Perhaps the most important feature in the new system of government aid is that the study circles, which previously received no financial aid, are now eligible for grants that pay about half the expenses.

A new departure is the short seminars with lectures and recitations, normally lasting about two weeks and dealing with a single area of study, such as a language, which are arranged from time to time in localities where the educational opportunities are limited or neglected. Free public libraries

(1 500), school libraries (2 000), and study-circle libraries (about 5 000) have attained great circulations and increasing significance. More than twenty million volumes were loaned to almost one and a half million readers in 1947.

People's colleges *(folkhögskolor)* are a type of educational development now receiving lively attention in England (cf. F. Margaret Foster's *School for Life*). They are an older manifestation of voluntary popular education than the types just mentioned and originated in Denmark. These institutions have made rapid progress also in Sweden and at present fifty-nine such schools serve as educational centers for their respective regions, enrolling more than 7 000 students each year. Their clientele is the youth from all walks of life, both male and female, their aim to provide a general education in the humanities and citizenship. Each of these colleges is an educational focus to the entire rural district that surrounds it. Some of the people's colleges are independent but associated with the province in which they are located, others are affiliated with one of the popular movements. Best known in the latter group is the Brunnsvik People's College in southern Dalarna, which is connected with the labor movement. The cooperative movement, rural associations, the Church of Sweden, nonconformist groups, and the temperance societies sponsor such colleges. These schools also attract foreign youth; students from eighteen different foreign nations were registered at the People's College in Sigtuna in 1947.

A statement made about the Workers' Educational Association, the largest in Sweden, may be cited as a general pattern for this whole movement in adult education:

"Like the British Workers' Educational Association, the Swedish Association is nonvocational, nonsectarian, and nonpolitical. This does not mean that religious and political questions are not studied. On the contrary, political science

211

and current events form a very important part of the studies. It does not mean that party programs are not studied; they are taken up in detail but always with an attempt at impartiality. Teachers and lecturers are requested to give a fair interpretation of the problems involved and to let the students know what are facts and what personal opinions."

By these and other means Sweden hopes to build an educated democracy in which each citizen has a grasp of the whole and a comprehension which enables him to realize his obligations to his fellow citizens and to society in its entity.

POPULAR MOVEMENTS

If a picture of modern Sweden is to be traced which might arouse some interest abroad, the popular movements deserve some special attention. The nonconformist revival movements were a reaction to the traditional character of the Church of Sweden; the labor movement rose against the impositions and injustices of the employers; the temperance movements rebelled against the excesses in the use of alcoholic beverages; the sports movements aimed for a more natural and active way of living; the feminist movement wished to enhance woman's place in society; the cooperative movement attempted to create a new form of economic self-help for the great mass of the people. All of these movements are responsible for invaluable contributions of the most varied nature which have in large measure helped to develop Sweden of today.

Since the nonconformist movements will be discussed in a separate chapter on religious life in Sweden, only the secular movements are treated in the present section.

Largest and oldest of the temperance societies is the Independent Order of Good Templars, founded in 1879. English and American prototypes were more or less followed in organizing this and the other important societies: the Order of National Templars, Verdandi, and the Blue Ribbon Society. With a present membership of 300 000, they continue to be an important educational influence in the life of the people and are distinguished by their interest in civic affairs and acceptance of social responsibility. Like the majority of the Free Church organizations, the temperance societies have lent support to the party most in accord with their program. Verdandi is on the whole social democratic or socialistic: a considerable number of Social Democrats are fellow members of the numerous People's Party adherents in the other temperance organizations.

Since the primary goal, female suffrage, was achieved in 1921 by the feminist movement, its activities have in part been transferred to the women's organizations of the various political parties. The pioneer work was done in the years around the turn of the century, but the background figure for the full recognition of women in public life is the talented and warm-hearted author Fredrika Bremer, whose travel descriptions of the United States *(Homes of the New World)* created a real cultural contact between America and Sweden in the middle of the last century.

Largest of all the popular movements started in the nineteenth century and least dependent on foreign models is the Swedish labor organization. The trade unions became the most effective means for joint action to achieve better working conditions. At first the union movement in the capital was politically undecided, but in 1886 socialism became the dominant political creed. This was in many ways decisive for the future, and the Social Democratic Labor Party was organized in 1889. Less than ten years later, in 1898, the trade unions consolidated into the Confederation of Swedish Trade Unions *(Landsorganisationen)*, abbreviated to LO. Progress was rapid and in 1907 LO counted 186 000 members. The general strike of 1909 caused a temporary setback, but the march was soon resumed and LO has today a membership of 1 218 000. Every ninth Englishmen and every sixth Swede is a union member, but only one out of ten Americans belongs to organized labor. Cultural aims are also included in the program of the labor movement, and its Worker's Educational Association is the country's largest. Most towns and communities have a People's Hall *(Folkets Hus)*, which is the center for all union activities as well as for cultural and social programs. Some of these halls have been decorated by Sweden's foremost artists. Several hundred structures of this type are planned throughout the country for the near future.

Labor organizations and their success inspired the formation of similar associations by farmers and salaried workers in offices, government bureaus, stores, etc. The farmers' groups are joined in a central organization known as The Swedish Farmers' Confederation *(Riksförbundet Landsbygdens Folk)* and under its auspices youth groups and educational associations have also been started. One of their main objectives is the betterment of conditions in isolated regions and they are, for example, erecting community centers for social life, clubs, and youth activities. In a country where industrialization is in steady progress the population movement from the farms to towns and industrial centers is not surprising, but ways and means of arresting the trend are being discussed and tried. The white-collar workers have also united in a central organization. Their earlier associations were consolidated in 1944 as the Central Organization of Salaried Workers *(Tjänstemännens centralorganisation—TCO)*, which has a membership of about 240 000.

In similar fashion, employers, businessmen, craftsmen, and the owners of small industries have formed central associations to protect and further their respective interests and programs. The cooperative movement (KF), which was discussed above on p. 107, also holds a major place in the list of popular movements.

Swedish organizations do not limit their functions to the recruiting of members for joint action and protection of their common interests. In recent years they have increasingly played a practical role in the life of the nation. When the government was faced with important problems during the war years, the organizations within the various societal groups—workers, farmers, industrialists—were sometimes consulted directly and thus recognized as factors in the life of both state and society. This was particularly true in respect to fundamental matters of budget and price control. Such a development is worthy of attention, for a part of Sweden's future is undoubtedly inherent in the organizations of her people.

SPORTS AND GYMNASTICS

In this connection, the sport and gymnastic associations deserve mention. The American traveller and author Bayard Taylor, who journeyed through Scandinavia in 1856—1857, amusingly and admiringly relates his experience with Pehr Henrik Ling's system of gymnastics in *Northern Travel* (New York, 1858), at that time a relative novelty. Since then "Swedish exercises" have drawn much attention abroad and inspired the origin of several other systems of physical training. Gymnastics continue to play an important role in Swedish life. It is a required part of the school curricula and many devotees use gymnastics both for general fitness and purposeful physical training.

Sports in general are of considerably more recent date. They came to the fore at the Olympic Games in Stockholm in 1912, when Sweden through good all-round performance and some luck managed to finish with the top score. Since that time, sport has become general and attracts young and old from all walks of life. Sweden has not been predominant in any particular event at the great international competitions, but the strength of Swedish sport lies in its variety and the firm hold it has on the country's youth. Sweden has produced outstanding performers in javelin throw, running (Gunder Hägg, Arne Andersson), swimming (Arne Borg), Greco-Roman wrestling, penthathlon (Wille Grut), association football or "soccer" (Gunnar Nordahl, and others), and skiing (Nils Karlsson). Soccer is very popular, and ice hockey also has many followers, both players and spectators. During the 1948 Olympic Games, both in St. Moritz and London, the Swedes achieved notable successes. Baseball, cricket, polo, Rugby, and American football are practically unknown. Some golf is played, and tennis has continued to increase in popularity ever since it was introduced to Sweden more than sixty years ago by the present king ("Mr. G."). The various sport clubs are now combined into a National Athletic Association with a total membership of about 600 000.

It is estimated that at least one third of the Swedish people hold membership in one or more of the various organizations outlined above. Those interested in becoming acquainted with modern Sweden would do well to use one of them as the point of introduction.

RELIGIOUS LIFE
IN SWEDEN

THE CHURCH OF SWEDEN

PROTESTANT NONCONFORMISTS

OTHER CHURCHES

THE CHURCH OF SWEDEN

In the provinces of Skåne, Västergötland, Östergötland, in the Lake Mälaren basin, and on the island of Gotland the small stone churches from the twelfth century and the ruins of old monasteries bear witness to the progress of the Roman Catholic Church in Sweden. The style of architecture frequently points to influences from England, France, and Germany. Early in the twelfth century an archbishopric with seat in Lund, then Danish, was established which for a while was the ecclesiastical center of the entire North. Its Roman Catholic cathedral was consecrated in the middle of the century. About the same time a bishopric was instituted at Old Uppsala in central Sweden. As previously mentioned, the bishop's church was erected on the site of the former cult temple, a location symbolic of Christianity's triumph in the very center of the old heathen realm. In 1164 Sweden became a separate archbishopric with the elevation of the Old Uppsala see. Toward the end of the thirteenth century the archbishop removed to the present town of Uppsala. At that time the construction of Uppsala's Gothic cathedral was begun, and relics of the sainted King Erik deposited there. His memory still lives, and the City of Stockholm carries his likeness in its coat of arms. The bishoprics of Skara, Linköping, Strängnäs, Västerås, and

Växjö also have traditions going back to the Middle Ages. Sigtuna and Saint Bridget's Vadstena, two towns that had great significance for the Church in the Middle Ages, have in our own century once more become religious centers.

The ecclesiastical unit corresponding to the commune also enjoys an autonomy which actually dates back to the Catholic Middle Ages in Sweden. The Church of Sweden assumed its present character in the sixteenth century when it became Lutheran and the vehicle of state religion. Foremost among Sweden's religious reformers was Olaus Petri, who had studied in Wittenberg under Luther. He is interred in the Stockholm Cathedral *(Storkyrkan)*, the scene of his preaching. His brother, Laurentius, became Sweden's first Lutheran arch-bishop; like many other outstanding Swedes he is buried in the Uppsala Cathedral.

All Swedish citizens, except the members of a few religious denominations recognized by the state, are considered members of the Church of Sweden. The activities of the Church are financed by means of income from church forests and other properties, with tax receipts, and voluntary donations.

The Church is under the direction of the government, parliament, the synod, and the bishops. The synod convenes at least every five years; it is composed of clergymen and elected lay delegates from all the dioceses.

Sweden is divided into thirteen dioceses, each headed by a bishop, an organization comparable to that of the Church of England. Uppsala is still the residence of the archbishop; the incumbent is Erling Eidem. The archbishop presides in the synod, in many of the national church organizations, and at the council of bishops.

Sweden is divided into approximately 2 500 parishes. Two or more small ones sometimes share the same clergyman. The total number of clergy serving the parishes is about 3 000, and one of their duties is to record much of the general vital statistics. All Church of Sweden ministers are educated at the University of Uppsala or the University of Lund. Together the two divinity schools have sixteen professorships in theology and about 500 students.

Central church organizations have been established for parish work, foreign missions, and religious and social work among seamen. Such functions as parish, youth, and Sunday school activities, publishing, newspaper, and study group work are directed by the Board of Parish Work *(Diakonistyrelsen)*, located in Stockholm. The Mission Board, in Uppsala, recorded 184 active missionaries in 1946. Missions are supported in the East Indies, South Africa, and China. Before 1940 the Seamen's Service Board *(Sjömansvårdsstyrelsen)* of the Church of Sweden sponsored work in twenty-five foreign ports. During the war the Swedish churches for seamen were wholly or in part destroyed in Rotterdam, Hull, Calais, Dunkirk, Stettin, and Hamburg. Within the dioceses are separate organizations for voluntary church work.

Swedish homogeneity in language and race is by and large also evident in religion. This is indicated by the fact that more than 90 % of the Swedes are baptized and married by the Church of Sweden clergy. However, these figures do not give the whole picture, for the Church of Sweden has acquired much tolerance since its strictly orthodox organization along Lutheran lines in the seventeenth century. Various religious currents and tendencies make themselves felt within the Church. Protestant nonconformists do not always sever their connections entirely with the official church. Many of those who are indifferent toward religion nevertheless observe the customs of the Church to a certain extent.

In southwestern Sweden a conservative Lutheranism is predominant. Strict church discipline and high church attendance are in evidence throughout the provinces on the west coast (Göteborg diocese), a situation traceable to the influence of Henric Schartau, a clergyman in Lund early in the nineteenth century. The parishes around Lake Siljan in Dalarna have to an extent preserved old church customs, finding expression, for instance, in the provincial costumes worn to the services and sometimes changed in accordance with the major church holidays. Various revival movements in Norrland that remained united with the Church have given religious life up there a certain Low Church character.

Early in the present century the so-called Young Church movement started among ministers and theology students, partly under the influence of the Christian Students movement. The Young Church wishes to bring about a revival of the Swedish church traditions and speaks of the Church of Sweden as a church of the people rather than a state church. This movement has received a lasting monument and a focus for its activities in Sigtuna. A number of schools and institutions for religious and cultural contacts have been established there under the leadership of Manfred Björkqvist, now bishop in Stockholm.

Sigtuna is also the location of an institute for the ecumenical movement. The late Archbishop Nathan Söderblom, whose work in many ways was of outstanding importance to Sweden's religious life, awakened a deep interest in the ecumenical movement among various church groups. Close connections are maintained with the churches in Denmark, Finland, and Norway. The contacts with Lutherans in Germany date far back in time. During recent decades the Church of Sweden has established closer relations with the Church of England. In 1922 the two churches agreed upon communion reciprocity.

In Sweden's religious life there are also some associations that work for a more liberal Christianity, others for closer adherence to the confession and the sacraments. Laymen's associations, people's colleges, settlements, youth camps for the various dioceses, and organizations for social service also enter the picture. Lutheran churchmen and Swedish nonconformists cooperate not only in ecumenical organizations but also in others, such as the Y. M. C. A., the Y. W. C. A., armed forces missions, and associations for religious instruction.

Adherents of political parties with a liberal or socialistic tendency have taken widely divergent stands on religious and church matters. At times the relations between church and state have been under discussion. It may be mentioned in this connection that Arthur Engberg, a Social Democrat and Minister for Public Worship and Education, rendered outstanding service in dealing with ecclesiastical issues during the 1930's.

PROTESTANT NONCONFORMISTS

In the eighteenth century the German sects of Pietists and Moravian Brethren (Herrnhuter) gained a toe hold in Sweden. The state church authorities voiced definite opposition, but it never came to the formation of lasting groups. However, Sweden's religious life was strongly affected by these movements. Beginning with the 1830's, English nonconformist influences made themselves felt, and during the latter part of the century extensive revival movements occurred, led either by laymen or by clergymen. Some of these movements remained faithful to the Church of Sweden, but many of them were separatist in character. The uneducated lay preachers were an element in the life of the Swedish people during the latter part of the nineteenth century, and Selma Lagerlöf included scenes with such a setting in her novel *Jerusalem*. At this time the first of the simple wooden chapels, meetinghouses, were built, which are maintained in many communities. About 5 000 such chapels and churches exist today, and the largest of the movements in question owns buildings in the value of more than 14 million dollars. Sweden's general social development during the past century and the United States contacts in connection with emigration favored these movements.

In the beginning the conflicts with the official church were many and serious. They were caused by the differences in teachings and other church matters, as well as by the law which until 1860 enjoined Swedish citizens from professing any other faith than that of the Church of Sweden. During our own century collaboration has been brought about and is now characterized by increasingly great confidence on both sides. Especially in the early days a fundamentalist tendency was strong in these groups.

Methodists and Baptists were the first of the religious movements. Inspired by their British equivalents, they came into being in the 1850's and 1860's. During the 1870's the Covenant Mission Church of Sweden developed from an older, Low Church movement and is today perhaps the most typical and also the largest of the nonconformist groups. The Covenant Mission Church comes closest to being Congregationalist in character. The three denominations—Methodist, Baptist, and Covenant Mission Church—cooperate with one another and constitute the oldest part of the Swedish free church movement, a designation which they themselves use. They have today a well developed organization with youth activities, Sunday schools, newspapers, a publishing house, social services, and foreign missions. On their staffs are about 1 200 permanent preachers and about 280 missionaries; both groups are trained in special schools for a period of three to five years. The clergymen of the Methodist Church share with Catholic priests and Jewish rabbis the right to conduct legally recognized marriage ceremonies. These three faiths have consequently made use of the right to establish religious bodies and obtain recognition from the state.

Several other religious groups of British or American origin have been formed. The Salvation Army has an extensive Swedish organization with seventy-five social service institutions. The Pentecostal Movement has found wide acceptance in Sweden and maintains large home and foreign missions. If the youth auxiliaries are included, more than 400 000 Swedes now belong to the nonconformists. In addition there are 250 000 pupils in the Sunday schools.

OTHER CHURCHES

The Church of England has congregations in Stockholm and Göteborg. Both the French Reformed and the Greek Orthodox churches have a congregation in the capital. Roman Catholics in Sweden number about 5 000 under the spiritual leadership of a bishop in Stockholm, who is under the jurisdiction of the Vatican's Department of Missions. There are three Roman Catholic congregations in the capital, one of which is in the charge of Dominicans belonging to the Paris province of the order. About 7 000 Swedes belong to the Hebrew faith, and Jewish rabbis are engaged in a few of the synagogues. About ten additional international bodies exist, but they are limited in spread and represented only by small groups.

THE CULTURAL HERITAGE

SCIENCE

NOBEL PRIZES

LITERATURE

THE FINE ARTS

MUSIC

THE STAGE

RADIO

SCIENCE

Scholarship, research, and science are traditionally honored and respected in Sweden. Early in modern times the Swedes were content to follow the lead of the Continent, but beginning with the Era of Liberty (1719—1772)—a fruitful age in science and discovery, whatever its political merits—Swedish researchers and inventors have made numerous and significant contributions to the advancement of science and its frontiers.

Olof Rudbeck (1630—1702), discoverer of the lymphatics, was the great scientist of the seventeenth century. In his *Atland* (Atlantis), a tremendous work, he represented Sweden as the country where civilization and culture originated. His opinions were at that time generally accepted, even outside of Sweden, and in some degree his views have been substantiated by archeological research in our own day.

Typical of his century is Carl von Linné, or Linnaeus (1707—1778), the country's most famous natural scientist, whose plant classification revolutionized botany. After his death Linnaean societies were founded not only in Sweden but also in France, England, the United States, and Australia. The London society is the oldest and best known; it is also the custodian of Linné's collections, manuscripts, and letters.

Disciples of Linné explored almost every part of the world

at his suggestion. They probed and reported the characteristics and peculiarities of natural history in Spain, Palestine, Japan, the Cape of Good Hope, and South America, to mention only a few. Among these scholars, Peter Kalm is familiar to Anglo-American readers. He spent some time in England and was the first natural scientist to describe large parts of North America (*Peter Kalm's Travels in North America*, 2 vols., New York, 1937).

Linné was one of the initiators and the first president of Sweden's Academy of Science (founded 1739), the institution which now annually selects the candidates for the Nobel Prizes in physics and chemistry.

In general the foundations for the subsequent scientific development in Sweden were laid during the eighteenth century, and her natural scientists achieved a position of international importance during that period. This applies not to Linné alone but to a number of researchers who were wholly on a par with their colleagues on the Continent and in many instances maintained close personal contact with them.

Among these outstanding scientists was Carl Wilhelm Scheele (1742—1786), who discovered oxygen well ahead of Priestley but failed to publish his findings as promptly. As a discoverer of new substances he has probably never been surpassed; his list includes nitrogen, chlorine, glycerine, and many organic acids (uric, lactic, mucic, etc.). By profession Scheele was a pharmacist and his work was done in the face of primitive equipment, lack of working space, business cares, and illness.

Also very prominent was Scheele's teacher, Torbern Bergman (1735—1784), professor in Uppsala, whose new analytical methods have earned him fame as the founder of qualitive and quantitative chemical analysis in the modern sense. His *Physical Description of the Globe* as a scientific work was far in advance of earlier geographical writings of a similar nature and was translated into several languages.

Sweden's outstanding astronomer in the eighteenth century was P. W. Wargentin (1717—1783), who in addition was noted for his work in vital statistics. Also widely known is the remarkable Christofer Polhem (1661—1751), natural scientist, economist, and technological inventor.

As the scientific development continued during the nineteenth century, much progress was made in the natural sciences. One famous name is that of Jöns Jakob Berzelius (1779—1848).

Berzelius, whose electrochemical theory is considered his greatest achievement, was the first to suggest that the Academy of Science publish annual reports containing accounts of progress in the various fields of scientific endeavor, an idea which was adopted later also in other countries. Berzelius may be considered one of the pioneers in atomic studies; as early as 1818 he published a table of atomic weights for about fifty elements. Furthermore, he is responsible for the system of chemical formulation now used universally.

Sweden has also produced several outstanding representatives in the humanities. Sven Lagerbring was an extraordinary exponent of historical studies during the eighteenth century. Johan Ihre is known for his investigation of the Gothic language and for his great Swedish dictionary. Erik Benzelius the Younger was one of the polyhistors of his age. During the nineteenth century, Erik Gustaf Geijer emerged as an outstanding historian; Oskar Montelius was an exceptional archeologist; and early in the present century the versatile savant Henrik Schück occupied a leading position in the humanities. However, Swedish studies in the humanities have primarily dealt with problems of national interest and have not claimed a great deal of interest abroad.

A near-contemporary of Schück was Svante Arrhenius (1859—1927), an important forerunner in the long list of modern Swedish scientists in various fields. He pioneered in electrolytic research and serum therapy. Two of his books, *Worlds in the Making* (1908) and *Destinies of the Stars* (1918), have been translated into most of the major languages. Gerard de Geer (1858—1945), geologist, evolved the geochronic system of prehistoric time determination previously mentioned. Manne Siegbahn (1886—) has made important discoveries in his X-ray research. The Svedberg (1884—) determined the molecular weight of more than fifty pure protein substances and during the war developed a process for manufacturing a synthetic rubber; he heads the Physiochemical Institute of Uppsala University. Allvar Gullstrand (1862—1930), ophthalmologist and physicist, brought about modern improvements in eyeglasses through his researches. Arne Tiselius (1902—) has made important discoveries in the field of chemistry.

A number of scholars have also established a reputation for their work in the modern humanities. Mention should be made of such men in theology and the history of religion as the late Archbishop Nathan Söderblom (1866—1931), Tor Andræ (1885—1947), Gustaf Aulén (1879—), Anders Nygren (1890—), and Yngve Brilioth (1891—), of historians like Harald Hjärne (1845—1922) and Lauritz Weibull (1873—), and philosophers such as Hans Larsson (1862—1944), Axel Hägerström (1868—1939), and Adolf Phalén (1884—1931). The two latter developed a philosophical approach at Uppsala which is characterized by strict, logical analysis. The list could be continued with such investigators as Martin P:son Nilsson (1874—) in classical archeology, Einar Löfstedt (1880—) in Latin philology, Eilert Ekwall (1877—) in English philology, Henrik Samuel Nyberg (1889—) in Oriental studies,

232

92. An apartment building at Reymersholme, Stockholm, representative for modern architecture. Photo by Gösta Lundquist.

93. The crematory at Forest Cemetery in Stockholm is an outstanding example
more recent Swedish building design. Its creator, Gunnar Asplund (1885—194
was one of Sweden's foremost architects. Photo by G. E. Kidder Smith.

94 and 95. The exterior of the new concert-hall in Göteborg. — The cooperatives play
an important rôle in Sweden's economy. Much of the food and the goods consumed
in Sweden is sold by the stores of "Konsum". The consumers cooperative also has its
own factories. Shown below is its Luma lamp factory in Stockholm, also representative
for modern factory architecture in Sweden. Photos by G. E. Kidder Smith.

Johan Nordström (1891—) in the history of education, and many others.

In medicine Gösta Forssell (1876—) has done successful work on radiotherapy in cancer, and Herbert Olivecrona (1891—) is a brain surgeon whose skill is becoming almost legendary. Another notable name among the specialists in Swedish medicine is that of the famous surgeon Clarence Crafoord (1899—).

NOBEL PRIZES

In the Introduction, we mentioned Alfred Nobel's magnificent donation, the income from which is distributed in November every year in the form of prizes to the foremost men and women in the realms of literature and natural sciences. A further prize is awarded the person who during the year has done the most to further international understanding and world peace. Many nationalities have been represented among the select few who have received this high distinction from the hands of the King of Sweden.

Since 1901, the year in which the prizes first were awarded, Americans have captured nine physics awards, five in chemistry, eleven in medicine and physiology, four in literature, and eleven peace prizes. England's share in the Nobel awards is twelve physics prizes, five in chemistry, eight in medicine and physiology, eight in literature, and six peace prizes. The English achievement is even more impressive if the whole Empire is included. — In 1935 the *Storting* gave the Peace Prize to Carl von Ossietzky, a German whom Hermann Göring in one of his speeches had branded a traitor. Hitler then decreed that no more Germans were allowed to accept Nobel Prizes "to prevent for all future the recurrence of [such] humiliating incidents."

Among the total of 219 Nobel prize winners since the first awards in 1901 the following are Anglo-Saxons:

Physics

Lord Rayleigh	1904
Joseph J. Thomson	1906
Albert A. Michelson	1907
W. H. Bragg	1915
W. L. Bragg	1915
Charles G. Barkla	1917
Robert A. Millikan	1923
Arthur H. Compton	1927
Charles R. Wilson	1927
Owen W. Richardson	1928
P. A. M. Dirac	1933
James Chadwick	1935
Carl D. Anderson	1936
Clinton J. Davisson	1937
George P. Thomson	1937
Ernest O. Lawrence	1939
Otto Stern	1943
Isidor I. Rabi	1944
Percy W. Bridgman	1946
Sir Edward V. Appleton	1947
P. M. S. Blackett	1948

Chemistry

Sir William Ramsay	1904
Ernest Rutherford	1908
Theodore W. Richards	1914
Frederich Soddy	1921
Francis W. Aston	1921
Arthur Harden	1929
Irving Langmuir	1932
Harold Urey	1934
Walter N. Haworth	1937
James B. Sumner	1946
John H. Northrop	1946
Wendell M. Stanley	1946
Sir Robert Robinson	1947

Physiology and Medicine

Sir Ronald Ross	1902
Alexis Carrel	1912
Archibald V. Hill	1922
Sir Frederich G. Hopkins	1929
Sir Charles S. Sherrington	1932
Edgar D. Adrian	1932
Thomas H. Morgan	1933
George H. Whipple	1934
George R. Minot	1934
William P. Murphy	1934
Sir Henry H. Dale	1936
Edward A. Doisy	1943
Joseph Erlanger	1944
Herbert S. Gasser	1944
Sir Alexander Fleming	1945
Sir Howard Florey	1945
Hermann J. Muller	1946
Carl F. Cori and Mrs. Gerty T. Cori	1947

LITERATURE

The partly versified text on the Rök runestone from the eighth century is Sweden's oldest literary document: difficult to decipher, it is one the most remarkable evidences of early Scandinavian culture. Saint Birgitta (1303—1373) has already been mentioned as the first historical personage in Swedish literature. From her century comes also the first rhymed chronicle, *Erikskrönikan*, in the romantic style then popular on the Continent. A poem in praise of freedom written by Bishop Tomas while the battles raged over the Scandinavian Union is still current. Its pithy sentiment that

> "Freedom is of all things best
> For man to seek in global quest"

had inspired several composers in modern times. In the age of Gustav Vasa the foundations for modern, literary Swedish

239

were laid by the Bible translation and the religious writer Olaus Petri. During the seventeenth century the literary ideals of the Renaissance found devoted followers in Sweden. Talented proponents of the French classical style and the philosophy of the Enlightenment appeared in eighteenth century Swedish literature.

A distinct place in the literature of the eighteenth century is held by Emanuel Swedenborg (1688—1772), well known especially in the Anglo-American countries. In the eyes of his contemporaries his fame rested on his scholarship and research. He was also well noted as a mystic, but only posterity has recognized his true greatness in this field. In many quarters Swedenborgianism is still a living force which also exercises an influence in literature.

Another unique position is held by Carl Mikael Bellman (1740—1795). The sketches of Stockholm life in his short songs, which he sang himself to the accompaniment of his lute, are characterized by an incomparable vividity and directness. They are full of esprit and feeling, alternating between joy and melancholy, a mixture of naturalism and rococo. Written to be sung, they are still on the people's lips today. French influence on Swedish culture reached its peak with Gustav III, the creator of a national Swedish opera and patron of literature, to which he gave royal sanction through the establishment of the Swedish Academy (1786).

A "Golden Age" in Swedish literature began with the early nineteenth century. Esaias Tegnér's (1782—1846) poems, translated in part by Henry W. Longfellow and many others, were written at this time, including the main epic cycle of Sweden, *Frithiof's Saga*. To the same generation belong Erik Gustaf Geijer (yā'yĕr; 1783—1847), poet, historian, philosopher, and an intellectual leader of importance; Per Atterbom (1790—1855), strongly influenced by the romantic move-

96 and 97. The annual award of the Nobel Prizes is followed with interest all over the world. Two Nobel diplomas issued to Eugene O'Neill and T. S. Eliot.

98 and 99. Sweden is rich in artists and authors. Most of them are little known abroad, but some enjoy international fame. Above: A portrait of August Strindberg by Richard Bergh (1858—1919). (In the National Museum.) On the opposite page: "Strömkarlen" by Ernst Josephson. A painting of a Swedish mythological figure, deeply rooted in folk tradition. (In Prince Eugen's collection at Waldemarsudde.)

100 and 101. Paintings by Carl Wilhelmson: "June afternon" (in the Art Museum in Göteborg) and Anders Zorn: "Margit," a Dalecarlian girl.

102 and 103. "The Egg of Columbus," a painting by Nils Dardel, who died 1941 in the United States, and, below "The trout fisher" by Leander Engström.

104. School class with its teacher visiting The National Museum. Photo by L. af Petersens.

A preliminary study by Carl Milles for the statue of "Carl Vilhelm von Scheele," in the National Museum. The larger, finished statue is in the little town of Köping.

106. "Skansen" in Stockholm, the leading open-air museum of Swedish culture. Photo by A. B. Refot.

ment on the Continent and author of the poetic drama *The Isle of Bliss,* on which Hilding Rosenberg has based an opera; the great hymnist Johan Olof Wallin (1779—1839); the enigmatic but brilliant Carl Jonas Love Almquist (1793—1866), whose fifteen years in the United States to escape a murder charge still are a rather unexplored period. His works have gained increasing recognition. Almquist tried his hand at every form of literature and in all of them demonstrated his significance as an artist. Erik Johan Stagnelius (1793—1823), a real romanticist, made lasting contributions to Swedish poetry before his premature death. He must be considered one of Sweden's foremost lyrists, gifted as he was with a rare ability to sense and bring out the genius of the language.

In some respects Viktor Rydberg (1828—1895) was an adherent of the romantic movement and combined its elements with a modern liberalism. Religious freedom was one of his main theses. His literary and scholarly production secured for him a central position in Sweden's cultural life toward the end of the nineteenth century.

Modern literature in Sweden begins with the emergence of August Strindberg (1849—1912). His life work is of the greatest significance. As a dramatist he is treated in the chapter on the Swedish stage; here we shall only list his naturalism, his impressionistic style, his subjective and almost brutal skill in placing social problems in a literary setting, his sensitivity, scepticism, relativism, and mysticism, all of which are found in his writings.

Ola Hansson (1860—1925) may be mentioned among the many important authors in the same period, that of Swedish naturalism.

Swedish literature toward the end of the past century followed the general trends in the literature of Europe, giving expression as it did to esthetic symbolism, patriotic idealism, and historical romance. The foremost representative here was Verner von Heidenstam (1859—1940), who presented his philosophy of life in both prose and verse. His historical novel *Karolinerna* is available in English translation. It may be said that modern lyric writing begins in Sweden with Heidenstam's collection of poems *Nya Dikter* (*New Poems*; 1915).

Selma Lagerlöf (1858—1940), story teller par excellence, (*Gösta Berling's Saga, Jerusalem, Nils Holgersson*) is undoubtedly the Swedish author best known abroad. Most of her works have been translated into a number of languages.

These achievements also coincided with a great period in lyric poetry. Oskar Levertin (1862—1906) was both a critic and a poet, a combination not unusual in Sweden. Gustav Fröding (1860—1911) is by many considered to be Sweden's greatest poet. His language is exceptionally musical: melancholy and humor dwell side by side in his view of life. The poetry of Erik Axel Karlfeldt (1864—1931), deals largely with his native province of Dalarna. He made effective use of the Dalecarlian concepts in folklore and art but was at the same time versatile in his interpretation and moved on a high lyric plane.

In the early part of this century the authors of the new generation began to devote themselves to the realistic novel. Some of the most important names in this group are: Hjalmar Söderberg (1869—1941), sceptic and chronicler of Stockholm life; Sven Lidman (1882—), novelist and poet in his youth, a moralist of note in his later years; Sigfrid Siwertz (1882—), dramatist and novelist; Martin Koch (1882—1940) and Ludvig Nordström (1882—1942), who were primarily portrayers of social conditions; Gustav Hellström (1882—), journalist and belles lettres author; and Elin Wägner (1882—1949), feminist and writer. A typical Swede was the great humorist Albert Engström (1869—1940), outstanding both as author and artist in word and picture.

The great genius of the present century's novel is Hjalmar Bergman (1883—1931). In numerous books, many of them very individualistic, he has demonstrated his talents as a psychologist sounding the depths of human nature, as humorist, depicter of customs and mores, and as a somewhat bizarre philosopher.

Birger Sjöberg (1885—1929), was a profound and original poet who in part followed a typically Swedish tradition in the poems he set to music.

Pär Lagerkvist (1891—) may be characterized as the modern, introspective thinker who is wholly preoccupied with the problems of his age and with the eternal ones as well.

Lyrists of note are Bo Bergman (1869—), Vilhelm Ekelund (1880—), Anders Österling (1884—), Dan Andersson (1888 —1920), Gunnar Mascoll Silfverstolpe (1893—1943), Hjalmar Gullberg (1898—), Bertil Malmberg (1889—), Gunnar Ekelöf (1907—), and Karin Boye (1900—1942), the last-mentioned one of the most prominent lyric poets in Swedish and also a novelist. Vilhelm Moberg (1898—) with his partly autobiographical novels that adhere to a popular tradition in storytelling, and Eyvind Johnson (1900—) with an output of high artistic quality and range are widely known and esteemed as prose artists. Versatile in both of these categories are, for example, Harry Martinson (1904—) and Frans G. Bengtsson (1894—).

A considerable number of the younger Swedish authors, from Eyvind Johnsson on, are representatives of the self-educated, so-called "proletarian" group who unaided and on their own ability have created for themselves a position in the country's cultural life.

In the prose literature, the foremost representative of the

women authors is Agnes von Krusenstjerna (1894—1940), who as a keen observer of human psychology produced her great series of novels on a lavish scale. As an example of the contributions from the so-called middle class the name of Olle Hedberg (1899—) deserves mention for his modern, rather ironic stories.

The rich revival of literature during the past two decades has in part taken place under Anglo-American influence. Since today's poets and authors stem from all walks of life they are able to achieve collectively a searching and comprehensive reflection of people and conditions in modern Sweden.

During the past decades a number of influential critics have emerged, many of whom are themselves at the same time active as creative writers; in a way this represents a tradition which started with Oskar Levertin around the turn of the century.

Program notes never replace the concert, and a brief account with a few names does not convey the value of a country's literature. Fortunately, an impressive selection of acceptable and sometimes excellent translations is available to the English reader. Reference can be made to the Scandinavian Classics, published by the American-Scandinavian Foundation, which contain many representative Swedish works, including anthologies of lyrics and short stories. Practically all the major works of such authors as Fredrika Bremer, Strindberg, and Selma Lagerlöf have been translated. Some translated titles will be found under almost all the authors mentioned above, except perhaps for the lyrists and those of most recent time.

THE FINE ARTS

A foreign visitor may most easily gain a comprehension of what Sweden has attained in the fine arts from her buildings,

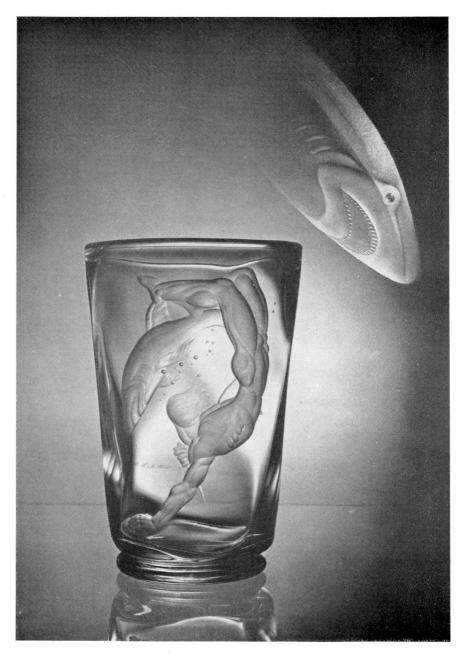

107. During recent decades Swedish artcraft has been in the hands of purposeful leaders. Sweden's glass industry, for one, is known in every country, above all through the famous Orrefors artists Simon Gate and Edvard Hald. Here is shown a glass from Orrefors composed by Victor Lindstrand. Photo by Orrefors.

111 and 112. Above, a modern room interior with furniture composed by Carl Malmsten, and a carpet by Märta Måås-Fjetterström. On the opposite page a cupboard by Carl Malmsten. Photos by Arne Wahlberg and C. Gemler.

116. Ceramic products from Gustavsberg, by Stig Lindberg. Photo by Gustavsberg.

ancient and modern, and from the treasures in the various museums. Old peasant culture may, for example, be studied in Stockholm's open air museum, *Skansen,* or at Anders Zorn's "Old Homestead" *(Gammelgård)* at Mora in Dalarna. Various types of farm buildings, textiles, folk paintings, and designs by country artists can be seen in rich selections—a living history of Sweden's past.

Another record, a vivid story of early Christianity, may be traced in Sweden's medieval churches; royal castles from the sixteenth century—Gripsholm, Vadstena, Kalmar—fuse Nordic austerity with southern renaissance and bring the imagination back to the Vasa Age. Baroque castles from the seventeenth century, built by wealthy noblemen, reflect Sweden's era of power and expansion. In the imposing, classical lines of Stockholm's Royal Palace we meet for the first time a nonanonymous, native architect of high excellence, Nicodemus Tessin the Younger (d. 1728). More recently Sweden has been noted abroad for modern and original architecture both in public and private buildings. Some of the Stockholm churches and Ragnar Östberg's (1866—1945) romantic City Hall have already been mentioned. The interesting City Library in Stockholm by Gunnar Asplund (1885—1940) has been the subject of high praise as well as controversy. He is the leading figure in modern Swedish architecture and has gained many followers who strive for an architectural style with a social emphasis.

During the intimate cultural contacts with France in the eighteenth century, Swedish painting received international recognition in the works of several representative artists. Some may with equal justice be included in both French and Swedish histories of art, such as Alexander Roslin (1718—1793) and Nicolas Lafrensen or Lavreince (1737—1807), others in Danish and Swedish histories, of whom Carl Gustaf

Pilo (1711—1793) may be mentioned. Elias Martin (1739—1818), creator of elegant landscape paintings, was trained in England but soon freed himself from outside influences to develop an original style. Karl Fredrik von Breda (1759—1818), a pupil of Reynolds in England, is perhaps best known for his portrait of Gainsborough. Johan Tobias Sergel (1740—1814) was Sweden's greatest sculptor of the period.

A new flowering occurs toward the end of the nineteenth century. Mention may be made of the pioneering Ernst Josephson (1851—1906), perhaps the most individualistic of the Swedish painters, who produced work of epochmaking importance. His last canvasses, originated during his serious mental illness, have recently been rediscovered and subjected to a new evaluation. Others were the gifted but excentric Carl Fredric Hill (1849—1911); the versatile Anders Zorn (1860—1920), who earned especially great esteem in the American art world; and a number of devoted interpreters of Swedish nature and everyday life, such as Bruno Liljefors (1860—1939), Carl Larsson (1853—1919), Karl Wilhelmson (1866—1928), Karl Nordström (1855—1923), and Prince Eugen (1865—1947), brother of King Gustav.

Most of these artists belonged to the Artists Association *(Konstnärsförbundet)*, which had a decisive influence on the development of Swedish art during those decades.

Great artistic activity, which to some extent observes the French trends, is characteristic of our own times. At least one of the living artists is internationally famous: the sculptor Carl Milles (1875—), who in recent years has spent much time and done a great deal of his work in the United States. Space does not permit more than a mention of a few modern painters whose work has been finished and therefore can be viewed and appraised as a complete whole: Olof Sager-Nelson (1868—1896), Ivar Arosenius (1878—1909), Karl Isakson

(1878—1922), Leander Engström (1886—1927), Gösta Sandels (1887—1919), Nils von Dardel (1888—1943), Isaac Grü-
newald (1889—1946), his wife Sigrid Hjertén (1885—1948),
and Ivan Ivarsson (1900—1939). A fine etcher was Axel
Fridell (1894—1935).

The Swedish museums are highly developed and enjoy strong
support from both the state and the municipalities. During
recent years a system of travelling exhibits has been expanded
more and more. Parts of the collections in the regular museums
are sent out as ambulatory exhibits all over the country, many
of them coming from Sweden's foremost art institute, the National Museum in Stockholm. More and more interest in artistic
creation is shown by the public authorities, by private concerns, and also by the popular movements. This is reflected
particularly in the outfitting and decoration of public buildings.

In the past few years there have been various indications of
a rising interest in art on the part of the general public. One
of its manifestations is the socalled "Art Club." A large number of such clubs have been formed by the employees in all
kinds of business undertakings.

MUSIC

Singing as a form of music, especially group singing, has
long been popular in Sweden. A rich treasury of folksongs,
augmented by more recent lyrics, has always given the university glee clubs ample material. From there popular group
singing has spread to the schools, especially the people's colleges,
as well as to many of the movements described in the previous
chapter. As a matter of fact, group singing is now almost

263

a "movement" by itself, although not as common as in England, for instance.

Sweden has usually been well represented abroad by singers of distinction. Jenny Lind Goldschmidt (1820—1887), P. T. Barnum's famed "Swedish Nightingale," was beloved on both sides of the Atlantic; for the last thirty-five years of her life she resided in London and was for some years professor at the Royal College of Music. Kristina (Christine) Nilsson (1843—1921) was the leading prima donna of Paris for almost a decade around 1870 and in 1883 sang the feminine lead at the opening of the Metropolitan in New York. In our own day a regular succession of singers from Sweden, both men and women, are heard in leading roles both at the Metropolitan Opera House in New York and Covent Garden in London. In 1947, for example, five Swedish stars were singing at the Metropolitan.

Interest in orchestral music was rather limited until comparatively recently. In the Swedish countryside, however, an astoundingly rich tradition of instrumental music has existed, surpassing even the wealth of the folksong. Modern composers have frequently acquired motifs and inspiration from this heritage.

Sweden has no composer whose fame abroad compares to Grieg's or Sibelius' of her more fortunate neighbors. Franz Berwald (1787—1868) wrote symphonies of high quality which deserve to be more widely known. The national trend which characterizes the postromantic music in various European countries gained its first significant proponent in August Söderman (1832—1876) and is represented in the next generation by Wilhelm Peterson-Berger (1867—1942) and Hugo Alfvén (1872—); the latter's rhapsody "Midsummer Night" is based on folkmusic motifs and often heard on the radio and in the concert halls. Wilhelm Stenhammar (1871—

1927) also belonged to this school in his earlier years, but his later work has a severely classicist, restrained character.

Tradition has been upheld by such composers as Kurt Atterberg (1887—), Oskar Lindberg (1887—), and, to a certain extent, by the highly original Ture Rangström (1884—1947). A distinctly modern tonal expression is used by a number of the present composers of the last generations. First among these is the very prolific and widely performed Hilding Rosenberg (1892—), whose outstanding choral symphony *The Revelation of Saint John* was greeted enthusiastically after its first performance in the United States (Chicago), 1948, the composer himself conducting. Among the younger ones the following may also be mentioned: Gösta Nystroem (1890—), Lars-Erik Larsson (1908—), Dag Wirén (1905—), and Gunnar de Frumerie (1908—).

Swedish opera includes the customary international repertoire, but a number of indigenous creations are also produced. Wilhelm Peterson-Berger, Ture Rangström, Kurt Atterberg, Gunnar de Frumerie, Oskar Lindberg, and Hilding Rosenberg have composed significant operatic works. Opera in Sweden harkens back to a great tradition with such world-famous names as Jenny Lind and Kristina Nilsson. In our own day, Swedish singers like Karin Branzell, Gertrud Pålsson-Wettergren, Kerstin Thorborg, Hjördis Schymberg, Jussi Björling, Set Svanholm, and Joel Berglund have become known far beyond the limits of their own country.

THE STAGE

A national Swedish stage in the real sense was not established before the end of the eighteenth century and then on the initiative of theater-loving King Gustav III. He was the first person in Sweden to realize the immense importance of a good stage in a nation's intellectual development. Not only did he introduce to Sweden the significant French drama of his time, but he also provided the stimulus for original attempts in Swedish, in no small degree through the plays he himself wrote.

During this time the beautiful theater in Drottningholm Castle was built by the architect C. F. Adelcrantz. Dedicated in 1776, it is still preserved together with its complicated operatic machinery. Also extant is a large number of stage settings with high artistic merit—a unique and valuable source for the knowledge of the stage in the baroque and rococo periods. Theaters were also built in the castles of Ulriksdal (1753) and Gripsholm (1787), both of which are preserved.

The Swedish drama of the nineteenth century followed to a large extent the path of historical romance, early introduced in Sweden. No first-rate playwright, however, emerged before August Strindberg (1849—1912). His dramatic works, chief element in his literary production, are uneven but include many great plays which have made his name one of the most important in modern dramaturgy. His influence asserts itself strongly in our own day, especially on the American stage, where it has been possible to carry out to the full Strindberg's scenic intentions.

In his choice of subject, Strindberg followed the tradition of the historical romance in his first masterpiece, *Master Olof* (1872). At the same time he breaks with that tradition both in the daringly realistic psychology and in the aroused outspokenness which give to the drama its vivid quality. Strindberg's subsequent production includes both programmatic and naturalistic plays. In the 1890's the dramatist passed through a religious crisis, after which he wrote a series of symbolistic pieces. They derive their originality and dramatic intensity largely from the unconventional realism which characterizes Strindberg's interpretation of the people he portrays. In no small degree those qualities are also traceable to Strindberg's language and dialogues, the latter uniquely fresh and penetrating. In structure and form these plays were the forerunners of the expressionistic stage in the 1920's, which was also strongly influenced by them. Beginning with the turn of the century and simultaneously with these symbolistic dramas, Strindberg wrote several plays with Swedish kings as the chief characters. In their historical interpretation these pieces are very subjective, but as literary creations they contain in their best passages a visionary suggestivity hardly ever surpassed in modern dramaturgy.

Both in Strindberg's day and later, Swedish dramatic writing has been rather plentiful, even though few of the authors have penetrated even by name beyond the boundaries of their native country. One exception is Hjalmar Bergman (1883—1931), whose works have been put on quite frequently abroad in recent years. While essentially a novelist, Bergman has in his plays furnished some brilliant proofs of his skill in picturesque delineation of human character. He leans somewhat toward symbolistic fantasy and has at the same time a sparkling humor.

Another successful dramatist in the present century is Pär Lagerkvist (1891—). He is practically the lone representative of the expressionistic drama and, furthermore, the creator of a new "idea play." Among the several others who should be mentioned in this connection are Tor Hedberg, Sigfrid Siwertz, and Rudolf Wärnlund.

The plays written in Sweden have never sufficed to furnish a complete repertoire for the theaters. The stage has therefore reflected the various currents abroad and has thus functioned as an open window to foreign cultures. This contact with the international drama has led to a number of interesting, artistically perfected productions, for staging and acting in Sweden have also been brought to a high standard through the active relations with the foreign stage. Among the American playwrights, Eugene O'Neill has been most frequently played, but also Maxwell Anderson and many others have had plays produced in Sweden.

Among the leading names in the present generation of actors on the Swedish stage we may mention Tora Teje and Inga Tidblad, both excellent character portrayers, Märta Ekström and Gunn Wållgren are also worthy representatives of this group. Anders de Wahl (1869—) has for two generations played with gusto the leading roles in both the classic and the modern repertoire. A genius on the Swedish stage and its greatest virtuoso was Gösta Ekman (1890—1938). Lars Hansson's (1886—) talent for acute phychological analysis has made him Sweden's foremost interpreter of Strindberg; Olof Widgren is an outstanding representative of the "middle" generation on the Swedish stage. Modern Swedish stagecraft is deeply indebted to capable and imaginative directors, such as Per Lindberg, Olof Molander, Alf Sjöberg, Per Axel Branner, Sandro Malmquist, and, among the youngest ones, Ingmar Bergman.

Swedish stage art is primarily centered in Stockholm. Here we find the Dramatic Theater, which besides its regular stage has an experimental one added in 1945, four other theaters with a dramatic repertoire, one operetta house, and a number of revue theaters. But Göteborg also has two theaters, each with a permanent staff of artists, an operetta stage with outstanding traditions, and a dramatic playhouse boasting a double stage and the most modern equipment. Besides other playhouses, Malmö has a municipal theater which is the largest and most modern in Scandinavia. New municipal theaters have also been built in other towns, such as Hälsingborg, Linköping, and Norrköping.

Not many are left of the formerly so esteemed private companies that were on the road in season. However, the Swedish rural districts need not be entirely without occasional opportunity to attend first-rate performances. Through the National Theater Agency, now in operation for about a decade, various arrangements are made to present plays in the provinces. Tours are scheduled by the Agency for companies from the national theaters in Stockholm, from the state-subsidized theaters, and from those under private management. In addition, companies are assembled directly by the Agency and sent on tour. Thus the country districts have a chance to see the foremost artists in excellent plays staged by Sweden's best directors. Every year twenty to twenty-five tours are arranged, staffed with approximately three hundred actors from the dramatic, operatic, and operetta stage. More than one hundred localities are played annually, and the number of performances per year exceeds five hundred. Where regular theaters are not available, the performances are arranged in other halls, such as the "People's Hall" of the local labor organizations, in the temperance society's auditorium, or during summer tours on an open-air stage.

RADIO

The radio has assumed a significant place in Swedish everyday life. The rapid increase in the number of licenses issued to radio owners shows the growing importance of broadcasting as a social factor. In 1948 they numbered more than two millions, and since 1939 Sweden has had more radios per thousand inhabitants than any other country in Europe.

The Swedish programs are largely planned along the same lines as those in most European countries. Included are entertainment of various types, such as concerts and plays, popular education programs, news and interviews, topics of the day, debates, and religious programs. A characteristic feature is the important part popular education plays in the total program plan.

The Swedish radio makes a specialty of interviews out in the Swedish countryside, where contact is made with people from every walk of life. This is done by sending out cars equipped with recording apparatus and staffed by reporters and technicians to all parts of the country. These programs never use scripts. The purpose is to induce all kinds of people —industrial workers, farmers, fishermen, lumberjacks, etc.— to tell about their lives, their occupations, and their ideas. By this means the Swedish Radio Service has succeeded in locating many people singularly gifted with a talent for narration. The recordings are preserved in archives and catalogued, thus making them available for research. Ethnographers and dialect investigators agree that this activity of Radio Service furnishes an invaluable record of everyday life among the Swedish people. It will give future generations an accurate conception of how people lived, thought, and spoke in our times.

Sweden's Radio School is conducted in close cooperation with the National Board of Education and has aroused considerable interest in the regular schools. About 300 000 copies have already been printed of the text book accompanying the Radio School's programs. They are at the disposal of any individual or group wishing to participate in the instruction.

Political programs always attract a large number of listeners. When hostilities ended in 1945 the political radio debates of prewar days between representatives of the various parties in the *Riksdag* were resumed.—The interest evinced by the Swedish radio in politics has been reflected in many other programmes. Great attention is being paid to the work of the Swedish Parliament, the Riksdag. In the recent past, Radiotjänst has received the permission of the authorities actually to make recordings of Parliamentary debates on the spot.

POSTSCRIPT

POSTSCRIPT

A visitor's first contact with Sweden is usually with the Swedes themselves. They were described long ago by Bayard Taylor, the American author previously mentioned, as friendly and decent, but stiff and conventional, with a weakness for everything foreign, and envious among themselves. He was struck by the complicated system of titles by which they addressed each other, impressed with the Swedish *smörgåsbord*, the fondness for schnapps and Swedish punch, the convivial singing,—and Swedish gymnastics.

While Taylor's list is limited, it is not too much out of date. Gustav Vasa is said to have described his Swedes as "a slow people, full of passions." Oscar Levertin, a Swedish author, wrote of the loneliness and eternal longing, which supposedly characterize the Swede, without specifying the reason for the one nor the object of the other.

More recent observers of the Swedes and their peculiarities like to pounce upon such matters as the alcohol restrictions and read in them an expression of stiffness and bureaucracy. Stolid, rational, shy, formal, generous, opinionated, cooperative, such are a few of the adjectives—good, bad or ridiculous—which others inevitably have arrived at when attempting to generalize about a whole people. All the critics should perhaps give the Swedes credit for an honest willingness to negotiate, a certain ability to find the way to a fair solution of controversies, and a readiness to test the conclusions by means of practical action.

These latter characteristics had a chance to develop during the long period of peace from 1814 to the present, but their origins are much older. In each century of Sweden's history something new has been tried and added to the heritage of posterity.

From prehistoric times came the skills in agriculture and iron production, the village community system, and the monarchy. Christianity was officially accepted in the twelfth century; in the thirteenth the provincial laws were set down, the king's council established, and, in the economic domain, mining and foundry craft were more fully developed. Written literature and the first written constitution were the contributions of the fourteenth century; the fifteenth gave the country a concept of Scandinavian coherence, a parliament, and the assertion of a national unity. The sixteenth century brings about definitive independence, a national church, and constitutional administration. Political horizons are widened in the next century, the people's freedom affirmed, and the national administration is further developed. New political activity stems from the eighteenth century, together with marked intellectual progress and a more equitable distribution of rights and privileges. The great transformation into a modern country comes in the nineteenth century with its land reforms, industrialization, popular movements, and democratic representation.

Our own century continues to build on these foundations. The popular movements have achieved a national basis, the constitution has become more democratic as modern parliamentarism definitely came to the fore, and the modern social system has been organized. Our present age has placed new emphasis on Sweden's traditional capacity to embrace new ideas and adjust to changing conditions.

Sweden succeeded in escaping the terrors of modern war, but the critical years of World War II have left their mark in the guise of new economic and social issues, new political complications, and new relationships abroad. Such complexities are not without precedent in Sweden, but they present a fresh challenge to her tradition of solving problems fairly and without strife. Most important is the feeling of kinship with other free nations which grew in the shadow of war. The long years of peace tended to nurture a sense of apartness, a vague but nevertheless persistent belief that Sweden somehow could escape the major conflicts and travails of other nations. Despite sincere and enthusiastic participation in the old League of Nations, that sense of separation hovered in the back of the national mind.

World War II has helped to shatter the old isolation. Sweden is finding her place in the international scene and today sees more clearly her part in world unity and teamwork. The nation is prepared to assume its share in the common responsibility of all countries to build a new world on a basis of trust and cooperation.

Location. Sweden is one of the northernmost countries in the world. Her extreme southern point is on the same latitude as the northern tip of Ireland and the southernmost part of Hudson Bay. Sweden extends farther north than Iceland and almost as far as Alaska's northern extremity. One seventh of Sweden's total area is situated north of the Arctic Circle.

Southernmost point: Smygehuk, 55° 20′ N. lat.
Northernmost point: Three-Country Cairn *(Riksröset)* at Koltajaure, 69° 4′ N. lat.
Westernmost point: Stora Drammen skerry, northeast of Koster Islands, 10° 28′ W. long.
Easternmost point: Kataja Island, below the mouth of Torne River, 24° 10′ E. long.
Greatest length, north to south: 978 miles.
Greatest width: 310 miles.
Time: Central European, one hour ahead of Greenwich.

The land boundary toward Finland measures 333 miles, toward Norway 1 030. The Finnish-Swedish border follows the deepest channel of the Torne and Muonio rivers, while the Norwegian-Swedish one runs over the mountainous wastes of

Kjölen, watershed of the Scandinavian Peninsula, down to northern Värmland, where it becomes a linguistic and cultural boundary rather than a natural one.

Sweden borders in the west on the waters of Skagerrack, Kattegat, and The Sound, in the east on the Baltic Sea, the Åland Sea, and the Gulf of Bothnia.

Area. Sweden includes approximately three fifths of the Scandinavian Peninsula. Her total area is 173 359 square miles, of which 158 301 are land, 15 058 water. Aside from Russia, only two of the other European countries have a larger area than Sweden, namely France (212 741 sq. miles) and Spain (194 208 sq. miles); the area of prewar Germany also was larger (214 672 sq. miles). By comparison, the British Isles (England, Scotland, and Wales) have an area of 88 803 square miles, continental United States 3 026 638.

Sweden's area and population may be compared with those of the three North American States Wisconsin, Minnesota and North Dakota.

	Sweden	Wisconsin Minnesota N. Dakota	U. S. A.
Area (1 000 sq. miles)	173	211	3 022
Land...............................	158	205	2 997
Water	15	6	45
Population in 1940 (in thousands)..........	6 356	6 572	131 669
» » » per sq. mile.............	40	32	44

Sweden is exceptionally rich in lakes and waterways; together they occupy 8.6 % of the country's area. Her greatest waterways are the rivers, of which twelve have basins with areas of 4 000—10 000 square miles. Ten of them are more than 250 miles long.

More than half of the land area consists of woods and hardly one tenth of arable land. However, the conditions vary in different parts of the country.

	Götaland	Sweden Svealand	Norrland	Total	U. S. A.
Area (1 000 sq. miles)...........	33	31	94	158	2 977
Whereof in %					
Forest	50	65	53	55	33
Arable land...............	25	14	2	9	17
Meadow	6	3	1	3 ⎫	
Unreclaimable, bogs, etc.....	19	19	44	34 ⎭	50
Population, 1940 (in thousands) ..	3 120	2 115	1 121	6 356	131 669
» » per sq. mile	93	68	12	40	44

Population. At the beginning of 1948 Sweden had a population of 6.8 millions. During the last century the population has increased by nearly 100 %.

A survey of the population and its changes since 1850 is given in the following table.

POPULATION CHANGES

Years	Average Population	Marriages	Births	Deaths	Birth Surplus	Emigration	Population Increase
1. *Numbers* (*in thousands*).							
1851/55	3 558	26	113	77	36	—	32
1876/80	4 500	30	136	82	54	14	36
1901/05	5 214	31	136	81	55	22	32
1926/30	6 097	41	97	74	23	5	18
1931/35	6 199	45	87	72	15	−5	22
1936/40	6 303	58	93	74	20	−3	24
1941/45	6 501	63	122	69	53	−7	60
1946	6 719	62	132	70	61	−25	90
1947	6 803	59	128	73	55	−25	78
2. *Per 1 000 inhabitants.*							
1851/55		7.3	31.8	21.7	10.2	—	8.9
1876/80		6.6	30.3	18.3	12.1	3.2	8.1
1901/05		5.9	26.1	15.5	10.6	4.1	6.1
1926/30		6.7	15.9	12.1	3.8	0.8	2.9
1931/35		7.3	14.1	11.6	2.5	−0.8	3.5
1936/40		9.1	14.8	11.7	3.1	−0.5	3.8
1941/45		9.6	18.8	10.6	8.1	−1.1	9.3
1946		9.3	19.6	10.5	9.1	−3.7	13.4
1947		8.6	18.9	10.8	8.1	−3.7	11.5

Industrialization has brought in its wake a heavy urban concentration of the population. As late as 1850, i. e. before modern cities and towns came into being, only one tenth of the country's inhabitants resided in towns. Since 1880 the population growth has largely been confined to towns and larger municipalities; in the really rural districts the internal shift from country to town ("the flight from the country") has brought about a population decrease.

	Population 1948 mill. inh.	%
Towns	2.9	43
Urban communities (of at least 200 inh.)	1.3	19
Rural districts........................	2.6	38
Total	6.8	100

In 1948 the urban population was distributed over 128 cities and towns, one half of which had more than 10 000 inhabitants. The largest of these are:

	Inh. 1948 in thousands		Inh. 1948 in thousands
Stockholm	703	Örebro..............	63
Göteborg	333	Uppsala.............	59
Malmö	181	Borås...............	54
Norrköping.........	82	Västerås	53
Hälsingborg	70	Eskilstuna...........	51

Ages and Marital status. In regard to ages the population was distributed as follows in 1945.

Ages	In thousands	%
0—15	1 456	21.8
15—30	1 492	22.4
30—50	2 036	30.5
50—65	1 034	15.5
65—	655	9.8
	6 673	100.0

In Sweden, as in almost all countries with western civilization, the birth rate has been on the decrease during recent decades. Sweden belongs in the group of countries where it has declined the most. In regard to the death rate Sweden is one of Europe's more fortunate countries. The productive work ages (15—65) at present include a greater number than ever.

The distribution of married and unmarried men and women is indicated by the following table:

| | Ages | | | |
| | 20—65 | | 65— | |
	In thousands	%	In thousands	%
Single........................	1 221	29.7	109	16.6
Married	2 693	65.4	298	45.4
Widowed	144	3.5	237	36.3
Divorced	59	1.4	11	1.7
Total	4 117	100.0	655	100.0

Swedes Abroad. Sweden's population would have been considerably larger by now, had it not been for the heavy emigration, especially to the United States, from the early 1860's to the outbreak of the first world war in 1914. During this time an annual average of 25 000 people emigrated, or a total of more than one million. Around 1930 the number of Swedish-born people residing abroad was calculated at about 730 000; those still Swedish citizens but living abroad numbered approximately 160 000. How these were distributed among the various countries is shown in round numbers by the following table.

If "Swedish" is taken to mean everyone of Swedish descent, their number abroad around 1930 was estimated at 2.1 millions, of whom about 1.5 millions were in the United States and about 60 000 in Canada. According to these calculations, the total Swedish population of the world amounts to 8.2 millions.

Countries	Born in Sweden	Swedish Citizens
European...............	85 000	46 000
Norway............	31 500	20 000
Denmark...........	31 500	11 000
Finland	6 500	5 000
Great Britain	5 000	3 500
Germany...........	1	3 500
France	1	2 500
Non-European	645 000	115 000
United States	595 000	95 500
Canada	34 500	14 500
Australia	4 000	1 500
All Countries	730 000	161 000

¹ Information not available.

Employment and occupational distribution. In regard to employment the population was distributed as follows at the end of 1945:

	Men	Women	Total	%
	In Thousands			
1. Employed..........................	2 240	752	2 992	45
In full-time occupation	2 103	740	2 843	43
Family members in part-time work...	137	12	149	2
2. Not Employed	1 083	2 599	3 682	55
Independents, without occupation....	255	265	520	8
Housewives.......................	—	1 335	1 335	20
Children under 15..................	737	709	1 446	21
Other family members..............	91	290	381	6
Total	3 323	3 351	6 674	100

The distribution of married and unmarried men and women among those gainfully occupied is indicated by the following table:

	In Thousands	Percentage of Total
Men	2 240	63
Married	1 366	91
Single................................	874	48
Women	752	22
Married	156	10
Single.................................	596	32

284

In the following table is shown the distribution among the various occupational fields of the population as a whole and of those gainfully employed.

	Total Population		Employed	
	In Thousands	%	In Thousands	%
Agriculture and related occupations	1 867	28	730	24
Industry and crafts	2 510	38	1 133	38
Communications...........................	525	8	224	8
Commerce	781	12	435	15
Civil service and the professions.............	593	9	307	10
Domestic work	161	2	123	4
Unclassified	237	3	40	1
Total	6 674	100	2 992	100

Income. The country's income distribution is shown by the following table, referring to those from whom income tax declaration was required in 1946. Those with an income below $ 164 do not need to file and are therefore not included.

Income Groups Dollars	Income Recipients		Sum of Incomes	
	In Thousands	Percentage	In Million Dollars	Percentage
164— 274	196	6.3	44	1.1
274— 548	570	18.2	232	5.9
548— 822	504	16.1	344	8.7
822—1 096	487	15.5	466	11.9
1 096—1 370	441	14.1	541	13.7
1 370—1 918	500	16.0	799	20.3
1 918—2 740	250	8.0	563	14.3
2 740—5 480	142	4.5	513	13.1
5 480 and up	41	1.3	431	11.0
Total	3 131	100.0	3 933	100.0

The average income within various occupational groups in 1946 is indicated in the following table.

285

Occupational Group	Average Income in Dollars	
	Entrepeneurs	of Employed
Agriculture and related occupations	1 168	666
Industry and crafts...............................	1 747	1 307
Communications	1 795	1 398
Commerce	2 431	1 386
Civil service......................................	—	1 687
Professions (physicians, lawyers, artists, etc.)	3 764	1 675
Domestic work	—	436
Unclassified	1 210	992
Average for all groups............................	1 529	1 230

Average Wage Income in Dollars, Including Periodic Wage Adjustments, Vacation Pay, Overtime Pay, Pay in Kind, etc., for Adult Men and Women 1946.

Type of Work	Men		Women	
	Hourly	Weekly	Hourly	Weekly
Mining industry	0.68	31.31	—	—
Machine shops	0.59	27.79	0.39	18.25
Mineral (except iron) and stone industries[1]	0.52	24.41	0.33	15.22
Wood industry[1]	0.50	23.59	0.36	16.43
Paper and graphic industries	0.58	27.50	0.39	18.19
Food processing industry	0.56	26.03	0.38	17.80
Textile and clothing industry...........	0.51	23.82	0.37	16.84
Leather and rubber manufacture........	0.55	26.01	0.37	16.69
Chemical industry....................	0.57	27.08	0.36	16.60
Building construction..................	0.76	33.89	—	—
Public works and construction..........	0.64	30.26	0.47	21.70
Communal works and construction	0.71	33.71	0.55	26.14
Commerce and ware houses	0.56	26.93	0.35	16.82
Communications	0.66	30.77	—	—
Agricultural workers..................	0.37	[2] 17.76	0.26	[2] 12.48
Forest workers (cutters)[3]	—	26.12	—	—
Gardeners...........................	0.41	[2] 19.68	0.29	[2] 13.92
Road construction workers	0.45	[2] 21.60	—	—

[1] These industries are in general located in the country, where the lower living costs cause lower wages as compared to the more heavily populated localities and their industries.

[2] The hourly wage multiplied by 48.

[3] Refers to the winter of 1946—1947.

Agriculture. Sweden is definitely a country of small farms. In 1944 they numbered 414 000, of which about three fourths had less than 25 acres of arable land.

Percentual Distribution of Farms and their Total Arable Land in 1944

Acreage	Under 2.5	2.5–12.5	12.5–25	25–50	50–75	75–125	Over 125
Percentage of farms.....	14.3	40.2	22.9	14.1	4.1	2.6	1.8
Percentage of arable land	1.3	13.4	19.4	22.9	11.5	11.3	20.2

Of the total population, 1.4 million earn their living from farming and cattle raising. The distribution is shown in the following table, where the absolute figures represent thousands.

| | Employed | | | Family Members | | | | |
	Men	Women	Total	House-wives	Children under 15	Others	Total	%
Entrepeneurs........	318	35	353	243	289	131	1 016	71
Administrative per-sonnel...........	13	—	13	9	11	2	35	2
Workers	239	10	249	53	72	11	385	27
Total	570	45	615	305	372	144	1 436	100
Percentage of total ...	40	3	43	21	26	10	100	

Use and yield of the arable land as of 1945 is shown in the following table, where the yield is given in thousands of metric tons and the area in thousands of acres.

	Yield	Area	Percentage of Arable Land
Wheat	588.3	721.1	7.8
Rye	276.2	415.6	4.5
Barley	168.8	230.5	2.5
Oats..........................	754.9	1 341.0	14.6
Mixed grain....................	462.7	685.5	7.5
Peas, etc.	33.5	63.5	0.7
Vetch.........................	6.5	11.6	0.1
Crops for grazing and green fodder..	—	291.1	3.2
Potatoes.........................	1 658.9	358.8	3.9
Sugar beets.....................	1 813.7	134.9	1.5
Root crops for fodder	2 107.8	162.1	1.8
Pasture and other crops............	5 537.3	4 253.8	46.3
Fallow and unused land	—	516.7	5.6
Total	—	9 186.1	100.0

The distribution of Swedish livestock as of 1944 is shown below.

		In Thousands
Horses		604
Cattle:		2 859
Oxen		3
Bulls		28
Cows		1 747
Young cattle		619
Calves		462
Sheep		558
Goats		35
Hogs		1 054
Chickens		6 175

The marketed cattle and hogs, calculated in slaughtered weight and millions of lbs., was as follows during recent years:

	1937/39	1945	1946
Cattle	289.3	208.3	245.5
Hogs	260.0	183.3	200.9
Total	549.3	391.6	446.4

Total milk production during 1947 amounted to 10 682 million lbs., of which 8 201 million lbs. were weighed in at the dairies.

Fishing in the Baltic and on the west coast adds a considerable increment to Sweden's food supply and toward the end of the 1930's gave occupation to 22 700 people.

Forestry. The conditions for silviculture are exceptionally favorable in Sweden. Productive forests cover no less than 55 %, or 86 500 square miles, of the country's area and yield timber of good quality. In 1929 the total timber supply in stands was estimated at 1 853 million cubic yards, of which 750 million cubic yards, or 40.5 %, were pine and 778 million, or 42 % were spruce. The annual growth is calculated at 62.4 million cubic yards, including 23.5 million cubic yards of pine and 24.9 million of spruce.

Two thirds of the forest resources are located in Norrland. Because of the climatic conditions the growth is slowest in the far north. It amounts to about 1.6 cubic yards per acre in southern Norrland, between 1.6 and 2.1 cubic yards per acre in central Sweden, and somewhat less in the southern parts of the country.

The tremendous importance of the forests in Sweden's economy is indicated by the fact that in the interim between the two world wars the export of forest industry products ranged between 168 and 189 million dollars, or from one third to one half of the country's total exports. Approximately one seventh of the national income is derived from the forests.

One half of the Swedish forests area is owned by private individuals, one fourth by commercial companies. The last fourth is divided among the state (19 %), the Church, the communes, and other associations, the latter three sharing the remaining 6 %. Most of the state and company forests are located in northern Sweden.

Of the felled timber, which in the 1930's amounted to about 69 million cubic yards annually, about 65 % was used for industrial processing, 29 % for household needs, 4 % in the production of charcoal, and 2 % for industrial fuel.

Industry. The number of industrial concerns, number of workers, and the production within the various fields of industry are shown by the table on the following pages. In the columns below, the industrial undertakings are classified in terms of workers employed.

Number of Workers	Concerns	Workers In Thousands	Workers Percentages
Up to 10.........................	13 617	59.9	9.4
11— 50........................	6 265	139.2	21.8
51— 100........................	1 038	73.1	11.4
101— 200........................	624	88.1	13.8
201— 500........................	361	110.6	17.3
501—1 000........................	123	81.6	12.7
Over 1 000.........................	46	86.9	13.6
Total	22 074	639.4	100.0

Production in the various mines during 1945, in thousands of metric tons, is shown by the following figures.

Iron ore and concentrates...............................	3 510
Pig iron	761
Blooms, crude bars, and ingots	1 206
Wrought and hot-rolled iron and steel	890
Cast iron	179
Hard coal...	615
Zinc ore...	59
Zinc	3
Lead	14
Copper	19

In 1945 Sweden produced 5 130 lbs. of gold and 55 409 lbs. of silver.

SWEDISH INDUSTRIES IN 1945

	Concerns	Workers In Thousands	Production In Million Dollars
1. Mining and Metal Industries	**5 631**	**250.0**	**1 025**
Mines.	114	10.5	36
Iron and steel works	58	29.5	173
Manufacture of iron, steel, and other metal goods	1 038	30.2	110
Machine shops and foundries.............	3 238	114.7	429
Sheet metal goods......................	532	6.8	24
Electrical equipment....................	253	26.2	103
Shipyards	158	21.2	74
Other industries.......................	240	10.9	76

	Concerns	Workers In Thousands	Production In Million Dollars
2. **Other Mineral Industries**.............	1 872	52.9	145
Quarries, etc.	501	9.0	21
Brickyards..............................	236	8.7	21
Manufacture of cement and cement goods..	356	5.8	35
Glass manufacture	129	6.0	17
Other industries	650	23.4	51
3. **Timber Industries**	4 217	69.1	268
Sawmills and mill works	1 688	29.1	118
Carpentry shops and furniture factories....	2 162	32.6	112
Other industries	367	7.4	38
4. **Paper and Graphic Industries**	1 280	63.0	368
Pulp factories..........................	79	16.1	119
Paper and cardboard factories	73	17.6	109
Graphic industries	711	16.9	87
Other industries	417	12.4	53
5. **Food Processing Industries**...........	4 884	55.1	984
Flour mills.............................	1 427	3.5	62
Bakeries................................	739	11.4	78
Sugar refineries........................	25	4.7	82
Breweries	489	5.8	47
Dairies.................................	871	6.9	279
Abattoirs and meat processing	504	7.1	161
Other industries	829	15.7	275
6. **Textile and Clothing Industries**.......	1 348	87.0	393
Cotton industries.......................	67	17.5	76
Woolen industries	103	12.1	63
Knitted goods mills	204	10.3	44
Cloth goods manufacture................	637	31.9	131
Other industries	337	15.2	79
7. **Leather and Rubber Industries**	834	27.3	143
Shea factories	273	10.1	44
Other industries	561	17.2	99
8. **Chemical Industries**..................	894	22.6	233
9. **Power Plants and Water Works**	1 114	12.4	153
Total	22 074	639.4	3 712

291

Electrical power, 1942

	Sweden	Wis., Minn., N. Dak.
total water power, 1 000 kW	13 000	—
installed capacity, 1 000 kW, hydro	1 978	436
steam	627	1 443
energy production, mill of kWh, hydro	9 230	2 427
steam	565	4 174
Rural road mileage, 1942	55 419	308 689
Rail road mileage, 1943	10 387	20 101
Number of motor vehicles, 1939	248 854	1 569 747
Number of telephones, 1937	724 595	1 100 016

Commerce. A very large number of private concerns engage in wholesale or retail selling and employ a considerable part (11 %) of the gainfully occupied population. In 1945 there were 318 000 people so employed, distributed as follows, in thousands.

	Men	Women	Total
Entrepeneurs	50	15	65
Administrative personnel	89	104	193
Workers	48	12	60
Total	187	131	318

Export and import. A survey of exports and imports during the years of World War II or the post-war period does not give a true picture of Sweden's normal foreign trade. The résumé below covers the year 1937.

Import	Value In Million Dollars	Percentage	Export	Value In Million Dollars	Percentage
Ore, metals, wire structural steel, pipe, castings	59	10.3	Pulp	114	20.8
Hard coal and coke	59	10.3	Ships, automobiles, electrical, machinery, ball bearings, motors	65	11.9
Raw material for textiles, cloth	59	10.2	Wood products, milled boards, box wood	60	11.0
Automobiles, machinery	46	7.9			

Hides, clothing, carpets..	29	5.0	Iron ore	58	10.6
Mineral oils	29	4.9	Paper, cardboard........	45	8.2
Oil-seed and oils........	20	3.9	Metals, alloys, wire, pipe,		
Fruit and berries........	15	2.6	steel	44	8.0
Coffee	13	2.2	Butter, pork............	18	3.4
Grain..................	11	1.9	Hides, pelts, and furs....	10	1.8
Fodder products	9	1.5	Matches	4	0.7
Tobacco	8	1.4	Fatty vegetable oils......	3	0.5
Fertilizers	8	1.3			
Wines and alcoholic bev-					
erages	5	0.8			
Total Import	582	100.0	Total Export	548	100.0

The following table shows Sweden's most important import- and export countries (the figures are given in mill. dollars).

	1938		1948	
	Import	Export	Import	Export
Germany..............	124.4	91.8	40.1	40.2
Great Britain	69.4	117.7	229.9	184.4
United States..........	92.2	45.2	188.5	80.8
Norway...............	20.–	33.4	42.–	100.2
Denmark..............	18.7	23.5	42.3	43.6
Netherlands	22.2	17.5	68.8	66.8
Belgium	19.5	15.1	79.5	65.7
France................	17.4	16.4	70.2	55.6
Poland	19.7	9.8	72.6	39.4
Finland	5.8	23.7	20.6	21.8
Argentina	14.6	9.5	29.9	42.–
Czecho-Slovakia........	12.6	10.1	30.9	26.8
Italy.................	8.5	10.4	45.9	24.2
Brazil................	9.4	4.7	30.4	21.2
Switzerland	10.–	3.5	23.8	27.5

National Income and Expenditures. The national budget for the fiscal year July 1, 1947—June 30, 1948 calculated income and expenditures as follows:

293

Income	Millions of Dollars	Expenditures	Millions of Dollars
Income tax....................	523	Defence	219
Customs receipts..............	64	Social welfare	246
Automobile tax	67	Roads and communications	82
Tobacco tax..................	101	Education and the Church.......	121
Alcoholic beverage tax.........	129	Agriculture	31
Other taxes and receipts	175	Other expenditures	122
Total	1 059	Total	821

Taxes. Direct taxes on income and property are paid in Sweden to both the state and the local units. The national taxes are progressive, the local ones proportional to the income. Since 1947 both have been collected at the source, i. e. the taxes of employees are paid by the employer, who deducts the corresponding amount from current wages. The amount of the tax can in many instances not be definitely calculated before the end of the year during which the income was received. The tax payer is then obliged to declare his income and property assets, on the basis of which the tax authorities establish the taxable amount. The taxes vary in the different parts of the country.

In Stockholm the following amounts are levied in national and local taxes:

Monthly Income Dollars	Taxes (per month)	
	Single Dollars	Married Dollars
55...............................	3.29	2.47
82...............................	8.49	5.48
110..............................	14.80	10.96
137..............................	21.65	16.17
164..............................	29.32	21.92
192..............................	37.54	28.50
219..............................	44.94	34.52
247..............................	52.61	40.55
274..............................	64.39	49.32
411..............................	110.42	89.87
548..............................	175.36	153.44

State-operated.

Entirely State-run: Post, telegraph, telephone, National Pension Scheme.

Very largely State-run: Railways, highways, waterpower, higher education, insurance against accident while at work.

Locally operated: Electricity, gas, water, sewers, stockyards, ports, lower education, medical care, care of the poor, child welfare.

Social welfare expenditures. The government budget for social welfare purposes during the fiscal year 1948—49 totalled $ 386.5 distributed as follows:

	Mill. Dollars
Peoples Pensions	153.2
Child Subsidies	119.6
Health and Medical Care	58.2
Family Protection	21.5
Child and Youth Welfare	3.1
Housing Assistance	9.6
Worker's protection	6.–
Employment Prevention	12.5
Miscellaneous	2.8
Total	386.5

The social expenditures of the local units and the district assemblies in 1948—49 are not yet known. In 1946 these expenditures amounted to $ 114.3 mill.

Popular Movements. The leading Swedish popular movements are as follows (political and economic organization are not included):

	Members
Sports organizations	640 000
Red Cross	475 000
Non-conformist groups	380 000
Temperance Movement	287 000
Tourist Associations	180 000
Women's Auxiliaries Corps	85 300
Scouts	83 000

The nonconformist groups, whose adherents as a rule have not served their connections with the state church, are nowadays generally recognized by the Church of Sweden. The most important denominations are listed below.

Number of Members

Covenant Mission Church of Sweden	106 000
Pentecostal Movement	100 000
Swedish Baptists	41 000
Salvation Army	36 000
The Methodist Church	12 000
Free Baptists	5 000
Seventh Day Adventists	3 000

Non-Lutheran faiths were represented in 1946 by about 5 500 Roman Catholics, 250 Greek Orthodox Church adherents, and 6 700 Jews, the figures including only those who were Swedish citizens.

The Press. In 1948, 239 newspapers were published in Sweden. During the first six months of 1948, the following papers recorded the largest editions, figures representing average number of copies per weekday.

Newspaper	In Thousands of Copies
Dagens Nyheter (P)	232 858
Göteborgs Posten (P)	210 057
Stockholms-Tidningen (P)	173 544
Aftonbladet (P)	168 950
Expressen (P)	133 152
Svenska Dagbladet (C)	90 734
Aftontidningen (S)	76 787
Sydsvenska Dagbladet (C)	62 987
Göteborgs Handels- och Sjöfartstidning (P)	37 947

P = People's Party, C = Conservatives, S = Social Democrats.

Tidningarnas Telegrambyrå (abbr. TT) is the newsgathering and disseminating press association of Sweden.

Tidningsstatistik Aktiebolag (abrr. TS)—The Audit Bureau of Circulations—founded 1942, is an institution, which every year audits the *net* sales and the geographical circulation of the newspapers according to uniform stipulations. This means that among other things both quantity- and quality-control of the papers are obtained.

Handelskamrarnas nämnd, Stockholm.	Chambers of Commerce Committee.
Svenska nationalkommissionen för internationella näringsfrågor, Stockholm.	The Swedish National Committee for International Economic Questions.
Landsorganisationen i Sverige, (LO), Stockholm.	The Confederation of Swedish Trade Unions.
Svenska arbetsgivareföreningen, Stockholm.	Swedish Employers' Confederation.
Svenska bankföreningen, Stockholm.	The Swedish Bankers' Association.
Svenska cellulosaföreningen, Stockholm.	The Swedish Cellulose Association.
Svenska trämasseföreningen, Stockholm.	The Swedish Wood-Pulp Association.
Svenska trävaruexportföreningen, Stockholm.	The Swedish Wood-Exporters' Association.
Sveriges träindustriförbund, Stockholm.	The Swedish Wood-Products Association.
Svenska wallboardföreningen, Stockholm.	The Swedish Wallboard Association.

Sveriges allmänna exportförening, Stockholm.	The General Export Association of Sweden.
Sveriges allmänna sjöfartsförening, Stockholm.	The Swedish General Shipping Association.
Svenska redareföreningen, Göteborg.	Swedish Ship Owners' Association.
Sveriges elektroindustriförening, Stockholm.	The Electric Industries' Association of Sweden.
Sveriges grossistförbund, Stockholm.	The Federation of Swedish Wholesale Merchants and Importers.
Sveriges industriförbund, Stockholm.	The Federation of Swedish Industries.
Sveriges kemiska industrikontor, Stockholm.	The Swedish Chemical Industries Office.
Sveriges köpmannaförbund, Stockholm.	The Swedish Retail Federation.
Handelns arbetsgivareorganisation, Stockholm.	The Retail and Wholesale Employers' Association.
Sveriges hantverks- och småindustriorganisation, Stockholm.	The Swedish Handicraft and Small Industry Association.
Sveriges lantbruksförbund, Stockholm.	The Federation of Swedish Farmers' Association.
Sveriges textilindustriförbund, Stockholm.	The Textile Industries' Association of Sweden.
Svenska lantarbetsgivareföreningen, Stockholm.	Swedish Agricultural Employers' Association.
Svenska lantmännens riksförbund, Stockholm.	The Swedish Farmers' Purchasing and Selling Association.
Jernkontoret, Stockholm.	The Swedish Ironmasters' Association.

Järnverksföreningen, Stockholm.	The Swedish Iron-Works' Commercial Association.
Kooperativa förbundet (KF), Stockholm.	Co-operative Wholesale Society.
Svenska reklamförbundet, Stockholm.	Swedish Advertising Association.
Svenska slöjdföreningen, Stockholm.	Swedish Society of Arts and Crafts.
Svenska stadsförbundet, Stockholm.	Swedish Town Federation.
Sveriges standardiseringskommission, Stockholm.	Swedish Standards Association.
Tjänstemännens centralorganisation (T. C. O.), Stockholm.	The Swedish Central Organization of Salaried Employees.
Riksförbundet Landsbygdens Folk (RLF), Stockholm.	The Swedish Farmers' Confederation.
Arbetarnas bildningsförbund (ABF), Stockholm.	Workers' Educational Association.
Folkrörelsernas rese- och semesterorganisation (RESO).	People's Travel and Vacation Organization.
Svenska turistföreningen (STF), Stockholm.	The Swedish Touring Club.
Svenska turisttrafikförbundet, Stockholm.	The Swedish Tourist Traffic Association.

SHORT BIBLIOGRAPHY

General

ASKLUND, ERIK, & K. W. GULLERS. Stockholm — The Summer City. (Photos.) Stockholm, 1947.

BERGMAN, GÖSTA. A Short History of the Swedish Language. Published by the Swedish Institute. Stockholm, 1947.

CHILDS, MARQUIS W. Sweden — The Middle Way. Third edition. Chicago, 1948.

ELDH, ARVID. Facts About Sweden. Stockholm, 1948.

EVLANOFF, MICHAEL. Nobel — Prize Donor: Inventor of Dynamite, Advocate of Peace. New York, 1944.

GULLERS, K. W. Sweden in Pictures. Chicago & Stockholm, 1947.

HEDIN, NABOTH. Main facts about Sweden. New York, 1947.

HULDT, ÅKE H. & EVA BENEDICKS. (Editors.) Design in Sweden today. Illustrated. Published by the Swedish Institute. Stockholm, 1948.

HÖJER, KARL J. Social Welfare in Sweden. Published by the Swedish Institute. Stockholm, 1949.

LAUGHLIN, CLARA E. So You're Going to Scandinavia. Second rev. ed., Cambridge, Mass., 1948.

LUNDQUIST, GÖSTA (Editor). Sweden, Past and Present. Illustrated. Stockholm, 1947.

MUNTHE, GUSTAF, & K. W. GULLERS. Gothenburg. (Photos.) Stockholm, 1947.

—— Sweden from the air. (Photos.) Stockholm, 1948.

PRINCE WILHELM. This Land of Sweden. Transl. by Elizabeth Kjellberg. Stockholm, 1946.

ROTHERY, AGNES. Scandinavian Roundabout. Ill. by G. Gray. New York, 1946.

SEATON, G. W. What to See and Do in Scandinavia. New York, 1939.

Stockholm, the Capital of Sweden. Pictures. Published by the Swedish Touring Club. Stockholm 1948.

Sweden. Pictures. Published by the Swedish Touring Club. Stockholm 1948.

GRIMBERG, CARL GUSTAF. History of Sweden. Transl. by C. W. Foss. Augustana Book Concern, Rock Island, Ill., 1935.

STOMBERG, A. A. A History of Sweden. New York, 1931.

SVANSTRÖM, RAGNAR, & CARL FREDRIK PALMSTIERNA. A Short History of Sweden. Transl. by Joan Bulman and published under the Auspices of the Anglo-American Literary Foundation. New York, 1934.

Anthologies

BANNISTER, ESTRID. Scandinavians Short Stories. London, 1943.

ERIKSSON, GURLI. Some Modern Swedish Poems. (In English transl.) Stockholm, 1939.

GANSCHOW, THEODORE F., Compiler. Memories of Sweden; A Collection of Its Best-loved Melodies with English and the Original Swedish Text. English Lyrics by Olga Paul. New York, 1937.

GUSTAFSON, ALRIK T. Six Scandinavian Novelists: Lie, Jacobsen, Heidenstam, Selma Lagerlöf, Hamsun, Sigrid Undset. Princeton University Press & The American-Scandinavian Foundation, New York, 1940.

HÄGG, GUSTAF WILLIAM. Songs of Sweden. 87 Swedish Folk- and Popular Songs. English Translations by Henry Grafton Chapman. (Songs of the People Series.) New York, 1937.

LOCOCK, CHARLES D. Modern Swedish Poetry. (In English transl.) London, 1936.

MANN, KLAUS, & HERMANN KESTEN, Editors. The Heart of Europe; An Anthology of Creative Writing in Europe, 1920—1940, with an introduction by Dorothy Canfield Fisher. (An Anthology of European prose, poetry and fiction in translation between the wars, with Sweden represented by Pär Lagerkvist, Vilhelm Moberg, and Harry Martinson.) New York, 1943.

Modern Swedish Short Stories. London, 1934.

OLZEN, ERIC, Compiler. A Collection of Scandinavian Folk Songs. Chicago, 1941.

Scandinavian Plays of the Twentieth Century. First series. (Four plays by Swedish authors: The Gallows Man: a Midwinter Story, by Runar Schildt; Mr. Sleeman Is Coming, by Hjalmar Bergman; The Man without a Soul, by Pär Lagerkvist; and Perhaps a Poet, by Ragnar Josephson. Alrik Gustafson's introduction analyzes each of the plays and reviews the field of recent drama in Sweden.) American-Scandinavian Foundation. New York, 1944.

STORK, CHARLES W. Anthology of Swedish Lyrics, 1750—1925. Transl. in the original metres. Rev. and enl. ed., New York, 1930.

—— Sweden's Best Stories. (An Introduction to Swedish Fiction.) New York, 1928.

Journals

Anglo-Swedish Review. London.
The American-Scandinavian Review. (A quarterly magazine richly illustrated.) New York, N. Y.
The American Swedish Monthly. New York, N. Y.
Index. Publ. monthly by Svenska Handelsbanken. Stockholm.
Quarterly Review. Issued by Skandinaviska Banken, Stockholm.
Swedish Foreign Commerce. Stockholm.

Bibliographies

AFZELIUS, NILS. A Bibliographical List of Books in English on Sweden and Literary Works translated into English from Swedish. Third ed. Stockholm, 1949, in prep.
HEDIN, NABOTH. Guide to Information about Sweden. New York, 1947.
A List of Books by Scandinavians and About Scandinavia. Selected by The Am.-Scand. Found. Fourth rev. ed. New York, 1946.
Swedish Books and Publications on Science, Medicine, and the Humanities. Publ. by the Swedish Institute. Stockholm, 1949.

Other printed or mimeographed material on various subjects is available and a list of titles will be sent on request from The Swedish Institute, Stockholm 3, Sweden.

INDEX

310

311